What

MW01138053

HEALING AFTER THE LOSS OF YOUR MOTHER

"Elaine Mallon has captured with word exactly how I feel. She verbalizes the pain of grief so eloquently. It's like she can see into my soul… the grief and pain. It brings comfort to know that I am not alone."

Michelle F., Surrey, England

"Thank you so much for this! It hits every feeling, emotion, everything perfectly. Like *yes… someone gets it!*"

Alice D., Palm Harbor, FL

"This is very well written and such a good reference to keep close at hand, especially during those very dark times."

Kathy M., Ontario, Canada

"Thank you, Elaine Mallon, for this. Everything you said is what I'm experiencing. Sometimes the pain is so deep and overwhelming that I can't even find the words. Yours help so much and are right on point. It's very comforting to know I'm not alone."

Laura O., Fresno, CA

"I've read and re-read this and it is still the *best* and most *accurate* words written on grief support that continues to help me."

Vicki G., Mobile, AL

"Tears flowing as I read this! Like someone actually understands!"

Joanne D., Ooltewah, TN

"Thank you for this! This is so helpful for anyone grieving. You have expressed it so well and it's the closest thing I've seen to an actual manual—at least one that is accurate and useful—on what we are going to be experiencing!"

Melissa H., Austin, TX

"Elaine Mallon, thank you. This is one of the most helpful things I have read so far. It has been five weeks since my mom died. I knew it would hit me hard, but had no idea how hard. I am pretty shattered and completely unprepared for this level of pain. Thanks for giving me hope."

E. Barrett, Brooklyn, NY

"This is the most helpful and beautiful thing I've read about grieving the loss of a mother."

Debbie B., Honolulu, HI

"I really needed to read this. I have no idea how to do this without her. Thank you, I shall read and re-read it."

Sally W., Glasgow, Scotland

"I really needed this... I really thought I was going crazy."

Rhonda S., Caldwell, ID

"All of the emotions described within these pages are exactly what I'm feeling."

Connie D., Winchester, VA

"This is absolutely the way my emotions have been. Thank you so much. I know I'll definitely be reading this a lot."

Nicky H., Albany, OR

"Reading this has helped comfort me. At least I know I'm not going crazy for feeling so empty and alone."

Kristi E., Salem, OR

HEALING
AFTER THE LOSS OF YOUR
MOTHER

HEALING
AFTER THE LOSS OF YOUR
MOTHER

A Grief & Comfort Manual

ELAINE MALLON

Library of Congress Cataloguing-in-Publication Data is on file in the Library of Congress, Washington, D.C.

Paperback ISBN: 978-1-7335389-0-9
Kindle ISBN: 978-1-7335389-1-6
E-book ISBN: 978-1-7335389-3-0

Story Editor: James Endrst
Interior photos by: Elaine Mallon
Elaine Mallon headshots by: Bradford Rogne Photography

Some names, discussions, and identifying details have been changed to protect the privacy of individuals as well as members of *Healing After the Loss of Your Mother – Grief Support*.

This book is a labor of love and is drawn from the author's personal experience. She is not an expert on grief. This book is not intended as a substitute for professional medical or psychological advice. Always consult your doctor or mental health professional for your individual needs.

Printed in the United States of America.

For more information, visit: www.HealingAfterTheLossOfYourMother.com

A Gift To You

To: _____

From: _____

Date: _____

Message _____

_____

_____

_____

_____

_____

With love and comfort.
You are not alone.

We knew and loved our mothers our whole life. It's no mystery why losing them hurts so much and why it takes so long to heal.

— Elaine Mallon

Dedication

*To my lifelong friend, Laura Hoffman Wilson: You were my lifesaver.
You were always there unconditionally with answers, comfort, and hugs
from halfway across the country. Because of your emotional presence,
I never felt alone in this.*

*To my mom, Irma: I know a mother's love is forever. So is mine. I also
know you will continue to love, protect, and guide me—that's just who
you eternally are.*

I am so proud to be your daughter.

Contents

Acknowledgment · xxi

Preface · xxiii

Part I: For Those Who Are Grieving · 1

Chapter 1 Your Mother's Death · · · · · · · · · · · · · · · · · · · 3

A Life-Changing Event · · · · · · · · · · · · · · · · · 3

It's Surreal · 4

The Five Stages Misunderstanding · · · · · · · · · · 4

First Comes Shock · 5

Then Comes Numbness & Denial · · · · · · · · · · · 6

There's No Right Way to Grieve · · · · · · · · · · · · 6

Chapter 2 Where Do I Start? · 7

Get a Support System · · · · · · · · · · · · · · · · · · · 7

Shifting Relationships · · · · · · · · · · · · · · · · · · · 8

A Compassionate Friend's Advice · · · · · · · · · · · 9

You Don't Need to be Strong Right Now · · · · · · ·10

Chapter 3 Cut To The Chase ·11

What Can I Expect? *The List* · · · · · · · · · · · · · · ·11

Chapter 4 How Long Will This Pain Last? · · · · · · · · · · · · · ·24

It's Different For Everyone · · · · · · · · · · · · · · · · 25

The First 90 Days · 25

From 3 to 6 Months ·27

6 Months to a Year ·27

The First Year & Beyond · · · · · · · · · · · · · · · · 28

Long-Term Adjustment · · · · · · · · · · · · · · · · · 28

The New Normal · 29

Chapter 5 Your Mother's Presence · · · · · · · · · · · · · · · · · 30

Present Tense · 30

Keeping Your Relationship Alive · · · · · · · · · · · ·31

Filling the Emotional Void · · · · · · · · · · · · · · ·32

Chapter 6 Grief Work vs. Allowing · · · · · · · · · · · · · · · · · 34

Surrender · 34

Releasing · 35

The Flow of Things · 35

Chapter 7 Grief Triggers ·37

Chapter 8 Holidays and Special Occasions · · · · · · · · · · · 39

Plan Ahead · 39

New Traditions · 40

The Holiday Season · · · · · · · · · · · · · · · · · · · 40

Introducing New Customs · · · · · · · · · · · · · · · ·41

Mother's Day · 42

Her Birthday · 42

Your Birthday · 43

The Anniversary of Her Death · · · · · · · · · · · 44

Making Things Your Own · · · · · · · · · · · · · · · 45

Chapter 9 Coping Tools & Strategies · · · · · · · · · · · · · · · 46

Mind · 47

Body · 55

Soul · 58

Chapter 10 The Emotional Pain Scale · · · · · · · · · · · · · · · 61

The Pain *Will* Lessen In Time · · · · · · · · · · · · · 62

Chapter 11 Grief vs. Depression · · · · · · · · · · · · · · · · · · · 63

Complicated Grief · 66

Suicidal Thoughts · 68

When To Seek Help · · · · · · · · · · · · · · · · · · · 70

Where To Find Help · · · · · · · · · · · · · · · · · · · 70

This Takes Time · 71

Part II: How To Comfort Someone Who is Grieving · · · · · · · **73**

Chapter 12 The Supporter · 75

Understanding the Scope of Loss · · · · · · · · · · · 76

Your Role · 76

Step One · 77

Be the Definition of Compassion · · · · · · · · · · · 77

The Gift of Empathy · · · · · · · · · · · · · · · · · · · 78

Sympathy · 78

Holding Space ·79
Grief is Not a Contest · · · · · · · · · · · · · · · · · · ·79
To Hug or Not to Hug· · · · · · · · · · · · · · · · · · 80

Chapter 13   How To Help ·81
Practical Help· ·81
Physical Comfort· 83
Emotional Support · 84

Chapter 14   What Not To Do ·87

Chapter 15   Practice Self-Care · · · · · · · · · · · · · · · · · · 90
Put Your Oxygen Mask On First · · · · · · · · · · · ·91

Chapter 16   They Remember Who Was There · · · · · · · · · · ·92

Part III: Grieving Community Forum· **93**

Chapter 17   Kinship Through Loss · · · · · · · · · · · · · · · · 95
Not a Club Any of Us Wanted to Join· · · · · · · · 95
The Power of Community· · · · · · · · · · · · · · · · 96
Online Comfort ·97

Chapter 18   Community Commentary· · · · · · · · · · · · · · · · 99
Common Thoughts· 99
Experience & Advice· · · · · · · · · · · · · · · · · · · 101
Positive Changes · 104
Hindsight · 106
The Time It Takes To Heal · · · · · · · · · · · · · · 109

Part IV: The Way Forward ·**111**

Chapter 19   Moving Forward is Not Moving On · · · · · · · · · 113
Does Healing Mean Letting Her Go? · · · · · · · · 114
Fed Up with Being Sad · · · · · · · · · · · · · · · · · 115
Intention to Heal · 115
The Power of Now · 116
Be Aware of Your Thoughts · · · · · · · · · · · · · · 116
Momentum · 117
Acceptance Is Not What You Think · · · · · · · · · 117

Chapter 20   The Way Toward Happiness · · · · · · · · · · · · · 119
Change Happens · 119
Release Expectations · · · · · · · · · · · · · · · · · · · 120
Accepting What Is · 121
The Way Through · 121

Chapter 21   The Path To Healing · · · · · · · · · · · · · · · · · · 122
Leaning Forward · 122
Final Thought · 122

Message From The Author · · · · · · · · · · · · · · · 125
About The Author · 127
Links & Helpful Resources · · · · · · · · · · · · · · 129

*BONUS: Your Personal Journaling Section · · · · · · · · · · · · · **133**
Notes to Myself: · 134
Favorite Stories & Memories: · · · · · · · · · · · · 142
Gratitude Journal · 151

Acknowledgment

"Your mother is always with you.
She's the whisper of the leaves as you walk down the street.
She's the smell of certain foods you remember,
flowers you pick, and the fragrance of life itself.
She's the cool hand on your brow when
you're not feeling well.
She's your breath in the air on a cold winter's day.
She is the sound of the rain that lulls you to sleep, the
colors of a rainbow, she is Christmas morning.
Your mother lives inside your laughter.
She's the place you came from, your first home, and
she's the map you follow with every step you take.
She's your first love, your first friend, even your first
enemy, but nothing on earth can separate you.
Not time, not space, not even death."

— Unknown

A special thank you to those who opened their hearts to me when I needed it the most, who shared their own experience with loss, who helped me learn, grow, and heal through their presence, kindness, and compassion.

Love will break your heart, but it will also heal it.

Preface

I'm not an expert on grief; I'm someone who lost her mom suddenly and unexpectedly. I was totally unprepared for her untimely death. She was beautiful, vibrant, healthy, optimistic, funny, and loved life. Genetically, she had at least another 20 years or more to go.

I was not expecting to get that call that February afternoon in 2016 and when I didn't answer the phone, my older sister texted me, "Call me now! It's about Mom."

My heart immediately sank. I made the call and my sister began as gently as she could. "Are you sitting down?" she said. "Mom's had an accident." My heart racing, I quickly asked, "Is she alive?"

She was—but she had been rushed to the hospital in Roseville, California, some 430 miles away from me in Los Angeles.

Our mother lived alone and had been found by concerned neighbors who hadn't seen her all day. They used a key to get into her home when she didn't answer, picked her locked bedroom door, and found her collapsed and unconscious on the bathroom floor. They rushed to her and immediately called 911.

It appeared she had either hit her head in a fall and been bleeding for some time, or had experienced some kind of non-traumatic brain injury, like an aneurysm, and then fell.

We didn't have all the answers. But it appeared she had been there since the night before.

Our mom was, however, still alive, though doctors weren't sure if she'd make it through the night. Her condition kept changing--showing glimmers of hope one minute to test results showing bleeding on the brain so severe that "she'd never be Mom again."

The fact that she was on life support and in a coma wasn't sinking in. No one actually used that word on the telephone. In the confusion, I just couldn't process the enormity of it all that quickly.

I was in shock. Numb. All I was hearing in those reports I was getting was that it was very serious, but my mother was being given oxygen and medication to keep her comfortable. My head stayed in a state of hopeful denial.

In my mind, if she was still breathing, there was hope for our larger-than-life mother. "I mean, she's *Mom*," I thought. "She'll get through this."

I rushed to the airport and grabbed the first flight I could get to be with her.

With my other sister, Cari, we sat with our mom as she lay unconscious in the ICU; we talked to her, held her and cried throughout the night.

By the next morning it was clear that despite being on life support, her body was shutting down. Our third sister, who had the extra burden of breaking the news to family and keeping everyone updated, was still in-flight and on her way.

We didn't know how much longer our mom could hold on or if our sister would make it to the hospital in time. All we knew was that it was unbearable to see our mom in such a state.

I never felt so helpless.

As we sat with her, I thought about an email my mom had sent me just days before asking about a friend whose mother was dying from a terminal illness.

In the email, she offered love and support to my friend, and wrote to me in her ever-loving way, "They are both on my mind today. No one wants to see their loved one suffer."

No, they don't. It's excruciating.

As my sister, Cari, and I sat with our mom, we told her how much we all loved her, but if she had to… it was okay to let go.

We held her hand, stroked her forehead to comfort her like she did for us when we were little, and we played her favorite song, "Happy" by Pharrell Williams.

A peace finally came over her and she took her last breath. At that moment, it felt like a part of me died.

Our mother saw us into this world, and with my other sister beside me, we saw her out. What a heartbreak and a privilege.

My world felt like it had fallen apart *like that*. A sense of security was completely ripped from under me. I was utterly heartbroken, shattered, and wondered how I'd ever live my life without my mom in it.

It just didn't seem real.

In the days after her memorial service, I had no idea how on earth I was going to survive this. I didn't know what to do or where to turn.

My focus was too scattered to wade through lengthy books or to hunt-and-peck for what I needed online. None of that worked for me.

Talking to people who'd been there was really the only thing that did.

This book is a labor of love and the result of what I learned through this difficult journey. Like a compassionate friend, my hope is that it offers the comfort, support, and answers you may need as you move through your own grieving process.

For those hoping to help a loved one navigate their way through their loss, I hope this may serve as a compass.

Right now, please know that if you are grieving, you are not alone. Too many of us know your pain and we stand with you.

We will walk this together.

Part I: For Those Who Are Grieving

"Grief is like the ocean;
it comes in waves,
ebbing and flowing.
Sometimes the water is calm,
and sometimes it is overwhelming.
All you can do is learn to swim."

— Vicki Harrison

CHAPTER 1

Your Mother's Death

They say your first love in life is your mother.

You literally come from her, and maybe that's why—whether it's sudden and untimely or expected after a long illness—her death is so colossal.

It feels like a part of you dies. It feels like a literal heartbreak.

Yet, a part of us heals just a little bit each time kindness touches our hearts. Compassion. Empathy. Understanding. Comforting words. A listening ear. Even self-care that allows these uncomfortable feelings to just be.

Losing your mother is a primal pain. I had known hurt and loss in my life, but I had never experienced anything like this. It hit me to my core. It was a searing, aching, overwhelming pain.

A LIFE-CHANGING EVENT

A mother's death is a major, life-altering event. It's among the hardest things we will ever experience in our lifetime. Everything changes.

I honestly didn't realize the depth of this, as much as I loved my mom.

I had true compassion for others who had lost their mothers but did not know anything about this kind of pain until my own mother died.

There is no manual for life and certainly no instruction book that prepares us for this day or how to get through it.

One of the first, raw words I spoke to a friend after my mom's sudden death was, "Where's the manual? I don't know how to do this."

The reality is we usually don't learn how to process grief until we are there.

It's Surreal

We don't usually think seriously about the fact that someday our mom really is going to die. Then when it actually happens, time stops.

It feels surreal.

Besides complete devastation, there are many common emotions you can expect to follow, but they won't necessarily progress in a tidy, structured order. Grief is messy.

The very first few reactions to loss, however, do seem universal: Shock, numbness, denial.

The Five Stages Misunderstanding

Most people are familiar with the five stages of grief, which was introduced by legendary psychiatrist Elisabeth Kübler-Ross in her ground-breaking 1969 book *On Death and Dying.*

It's a commonly accepted belief that grief proceeds in stages. But the five stages—denial, anger, bargaining, depression, and acceptance--were meant to describe the emotional progression of people who are coping with illness and dying. *They were never intended to describe or reflect on how a person grieves.*

"The stages have evolved since their introduction, and they have been misunderstood over the past three decades," Dr. Kübler-Ross' writes in her last book, *On Grief and Grieving*, co-authored by her collaborator and grief expert David Kessler.

The book explains that the stages are "tools to help us frame and identify what we may be feeling. But they are not stops on some linear timeline in grief. Not everyone goes through all of them or goes in a prescribed order."

The fact is, there is no orderly progression through grief and grieving. It's as individual as we are.

When it comes to grief, it may help us to think of the stages, then, as a general framework of what to expect—not an organized list you can check off and be done with.

FIRST COMES SHOCK

Regardless of the individual, the initial response to your mother's death is usually shock.

Shock is the body's way of protecting us when too much information could overload our nervous system. It's our natural defense mechanism until we can catch up with reality.

Then Comes Numbness & Denial

Shock is often closely followed by numbness and denial.

"Denial serves a valuable purpose to keep the psyche safe before the person is ready to deal with the reality," explains Tamaara Smith, a certified master practitioner of neurolinguistic programming (NLP), who coaches individuals through grief and major life transitions.

The mix of information and intense emotions are a lot to process at once. Your mind races to try to make sense of things. "No," it says. "How can this be? This doesn't seem real."

Denial is a buffer zone between what has happened and reality that can linger for days or years. Sometimes, a mother's death is too much to accept and many find it easier to put it on a shelf to cope with later.

As the numbness starts to wear off and the reality settles in, a tidal wave of emotions hit… *and it doesn't feel real.*

There's No Right Way To Grieve

This is new territory for most people. We live in a culture that doesn't really talk about the true scope of grief, especially about how deeply the death of one's mother affects a person.

You may worry, "Am I doing this right?"

Most people are relieved to learn that there is no right or wrong way to grieve. The process is entirely personal and your own. That's a promise echoed in bereavement support groups, by doctors and from others who have been there.

You cannot get it wrong and there's no such thing as "right."

The best you can do is to be patient with yourself, follow your feelings and keep your heart open as you move through grief.

CHAPTER 2

Where Do I Start?

GET A SUPPORT SYSTEM

The first person I reached out to for help and comfort was my best friend since childhood, Laura, who now lives halfway across the country in Texas.

After a 45-year friendship, she knew not only my heart, but she knew my mom and could understand better than anyone my shock and utter heartbreak.

Plus, she had lost her own father a decade before and knew not only the pain but what to expect.

When I cried, she did too, because she could understand my loss on every level. She never pushed me, always listened, gave gentle support, and thoughtful nurturing. She had compassion.

When I was too emotionally and physically exhausted to cook for myself or make myself eat, she ordered food delivered from my favorite restaurant. She made sure I felt nurtured and that I kept my strength up—even if she couldn't be there with me.

Someone doesn't have to be physically with you to be emotionally there for you. They just need to be *present*.

It's so valuable to have at least one person like this to turn to. (If not more.) If they don't know your history, just being around heart-centered people helps tremendously.

When family or friends can't relate to this kind of loss, there are other resources who do get it and can be of great help.

Most places of worship and hospitals offer grief support groups, and there are also many online groups that can add to your system of support.

Social workers, counselors who specialize in bereavement, grief coaches and other professionals are out there to help as well.

SHIFTING RELATIONSHIPS

As you move through grief, relationships may shift. This is a time when you need to be what some *may* consider "selfish." It's really about practicing "self-care."

I found that you need to put your healing first.

All the energy that would otherwise be focused outward toward others needs to go inward as you put *you* back together again.

The people in your life will either adjust to the *new you* as you work through this or they may go away. The conditional relationships in your life will start to reveal themselves.

Some may not like the changes you are going through. Some may not understand. They may resent that you are not there for them like before. Maybe your role was to be "the giver," "the patient listener," "the partner in crime."

As you change and grow, you need to be around people who will support that. If someone accuses you of being selfish, it could actually be they're upset that *their* needs aren't being met like before.

Some people may not want to stick around. Whatever they choose, let them.

Now is the time to lean on people who have your back *and* your heart.

A Compassionate Friend's Advice

My friend Laura gave me some of the best advice right up front. She told me:

* "No one can tell you how to grieve."

* "You can't put a timeline on grief. You have to take it at your own pace."

* "It took a lifetime to build the memories you have with your mom; it will naturally take a lot of time to mourn her loss in your life."

* "People who unconditionally love you will understand if you're having a hard time and not at your best right now. If they don't support you through this, step away from them."

❧ "The pain will come in waves—sometimes tidal waves— but will lessen over time."

❧ "This is one of the most difficult things we will go through in our lives, but we do get through it."

You Don't Need To Be Strong Right Now

Early on, I remember hearing a true story in a grief support group about an older lady who came up to a woman while she was crying at her mother's grave.

To paraphrase it, the sweet stranger leaned over and gently told her:

"People will tell you to be strong. Ignore them. You are allowed to fall apart, feel bad, and struggle because when you need to be strong again, you will be. For now, cry. Be sad. Be angry. Go ahead and fall apart because that's how you become whole again."

That story made an impression on me when I was flailing about with so many uncomfortable and overpowering emotions. It gave me the *permission* to fall apart and validated everything I was feeling.

You have permission to grieve in any way you need to right now. It's how we heal.

CHAPTER 3

Cut To The Chase

In the beginning, I didn't want cliché words of sympathy. What I needed was someone to tell me what I should expect to happen and how I was supposed to get through this.

I wanted someone to give it to me straight.

WHAT CAN I EXPECT? *THE LIST*

Here are the key lessons I learned that I hope will help:

* There is no timeline.

* Grief is not linear.

* No one can tell you how to mourn or when to stop.

* Losing your mother hits hard, no matter how prepared you might be.

* You are left raw.

* It can feel soul-crushing.

* Your world may suddenly feel as if it's been turned upside down.

* It affects your mental, physical, and spiritual bodies.

* As noted earlier, throw the five stages of grief out the window. There's no roadmap; no orderly progression through this—people who are grieving usually experience some or all of those emotions and many more.

* You can expect a roller coaster ride of emotions through shock, numbness, sadness, anger, irritability, guilt, regret, depression, despair and more.

* Emotions may change day to day, and sometimes hour to hour or minute by minute.

* There's no predictability to the process. You may be thinking you've managed a particular emotion one moment, just to re-experience it again later... sometimes, again and again.

* Get ready for a lot of spontaneous weeping.

* You may feel like you're losing your mind. You're not crazy. You're grieving. (I thought I was going cuckoo.)

* You may find yourself reacting in ways that may even shock you. Anger, early on, is a big one. The flood of emotions may feel like a shock to your nervous system. (I felt like mine had been fried.) That surge of emotions will need to work their way out of your body and they come up to be released.

* Mood swings are an expected part of the process.

* You may be short on patience. Even simple pleasantries can annoy you.

* Grief experts say emotions are layered. Beneath anger is pain. Your pain of sadness and loss.

* While we all experience grief differently, we also *express* grief in our own ways. Some people's sadness or anger may appear to be more pronounced; others may internalize their feelings and keep their grief to themselves. Both can be grieving just as deeply.

* Emotional pain can be just as debilitating as physical pain, you just don't see a cast or bandage. Healing takes time in both cases.

* Physical symptoms of grief can include: Fatigue, anxiety, headaches, aches and pains, shortness of breath, cognitive issues, appetite loss, and a weakened immune system.

* In the beginning, grief can feel all-consuming. It's on your mind 24/7.

* You may grieve for your mother, your childhood, your sense of security in the world and the family you once were.

* You may feel alone even in the company of others.

* Inside, you may feel empty.

* Regardless of age, you may feel like a little kid again aching for your mom.

* It's very common to feel detached, not like "you" as you process so many emotions. (I felt like an alien in my own body.)

* It can feel overwhelming on so many levels. First, in losing her, then in feeling like you're losing yourself.

* You may struggle with what feels like an identity crisis. It's a natural shift as you wonder: "Who am I without my mother?"

* It's natural to have regrets—things you wish you had said or done, as well as things you wish you hadn't said or done.

* You wonder if you will ever feel joy again. (You will.)

* There is a need to isolate.

* Focusing is hard.

* What really matters in life really gets put into focus fast.

* Many mornings you may wake up and feel that everything is like it was before for a few sleepy moments until you realize again that she's gone.

* You will certainly miss the physical presence of your mother, but you will also long for the essence of who she was in your life.

* You may begin to obsess about your own safety, security, and death.

* As you realize the unthinkable *can* happen, you may begin to worry about the mortality of others you love as well.

* You can try to cover all this pain up or temporarily soothe yourself with drugs, alcohol, shopping, or any distraction so you don't feel the uncomfortable feelings. Be aware that that can make things worse. It also delays the healing process.

* Still, don't beat yourself up if you can't face reality just yet. Be gentle with yourself. This isn't about perfection; it's about surviving and doing the best you can.

* Your sleep patterns may change. Bouts of insomnia are common.

* You may find yourself suddenly very accident-prone. You are more likely to be more in your head and out-of-body. Be especially careful when driving.

* Fleeting suicidal thoughts are not uncommon. If they do occur, talk to someone or seek professional help.

* Allowing professional guidance is important when you need extra support. That is practicing self-care.

* You feel powerless to the whole process.

* You may try to control whatever areas of your life you have at least some control over.

* With so much uncertainty in your life right now, you may become more sensitive—and less tolerant of—those who run late or cancel plans on you. There is a strong need for reliability and consistency. It lends some sense of security when little else does.

* You question the meaning of life.

* With so many unknowns, there is a constant fear of the next shoe dropping.

* You will probably feel "messed up" for some time. Just remember, that's what grief looks like. Try not to judge yourself—grief packs a wallop.

* The loss is made harder by the realization that your mother will not be present in important moments of your life going forward. (Marriages, births, milestones, and celebrations.)

* Holidays and birthdays are dreaded by those in grief.

* You may begin to look at life differently—change your priorities and reassess your life purpose.

* You may suddenly become acutely aware of the value of time and the preciousness of life.

* Your family dynamics may change.

* Grief is stressful for the whole family. Roles change. People cope differently. Misunderstandings are common. Whatever cracks there were in the family foundation before your mother's passing may become even bigger.

* If your mom was "the glue" of the family, things can fall apart. When this happens, it feels like a secondary loss to grieve.

* You may start to question your faith or explore new ones.

- It's common to play the last days, weeks, or moments of your mother's passing in a loop in your head.

- There may also be unending questions that are difficult to make sense of as your mind tries to catch up with reality. Experts assure it's a part of processing the trauma.

- It's common to feel abandoned in some way: lost without the security of your mother.

- If your mother meant "home" to you, you may suddenly feel homeless.

- Making simple decisions can feel overwhelming.

- Try not to make any big decisions (moving, changing major relationships, changing your job, especially major financial decisions) in the first several months to a year until your emotions are more settled and your mind is less foggy.

- Many note, with some sensitivity, the day of the week their mother died. In the beginning, you may feel anxious and dread each time when that day of the week arrives.

- When you know what to expect, it's easier to step back and let whatever comes up just be. You will see that feelings do pass.

The first three months are the hardest. The pain hits like a crushing tsunami. You may wonder how you will survive this, but please know the intensity you feel in the beginning won't last forever. It *will* ease in time.

As grief does its thing, you just need to hold on as you work through the many adjustments it brings:

◆ Remember to breathe.

◆ Self-care is key.

◆ You can't rush the process.

◆ Try not to take on too much. It's okay to say no.

◆ Resist judging your emotions or comparing yourself to others.

◆ It's quite common to feel twinges of jealousy or envy when you see mothers and daughters or sons together. You're not being petty, you're in pain.

◆ It's suddenly very difficult, if not maddening, to hear people complain about their mothers. It's common to want to say, "At least you have a mother."

◆ Grief can feel exhausting. Just when you think you might be through it, another wave may hit you.

◆ A *grief ambush* may hit at any time and by total surprise. One minute you may be watering the garden and the next moment bursting into tears. It just sneaks up on you.

* You may walk around looking normal on the outside, but empty of anything and having pain and emotional exhaustion on the inside. You feel like a *grief zombie.*

* Grief may burrow in deep if you ignore it, only to come up in explosive or surprising ways later.

* You may see someone who reminds you of your mother. It may stop you in your tracks. Your heart may race. You might tear up or have the urge to go hug her.

* You get good at wearing the "grief mask". One face has it together for the outside world, but underneath you're falling apart.

* It can feel comforting to see her handwriting. It's a tangible piece of her she leaves behind.

* Wearing or touching her clothes or jewelry also makes you feel close to her.

* Most say to themselves, "I just want to feel normal again."

Besides the emotional, physical, mental, and spiritual ways grief affects a person's life, it also can affect how you interact with others.

Even the most outgoing people can suddenly feel uneasy in social settings. It helps to be honest with others about how you're feeling or what you need.

Chances are they don't know, and you may be reassured you have nothing to be ashamed of.

Things are just easier when you don't put expectations on yourself to be anything other than who you are, wherever you are in the process.

Some ways grief can affect your social life include:

* You may just prefer to be alone, even if you miss being around others. Socializing takes a lot of effort.

* It's hard to make plans because you can't predict how you might be feeling when the event comes.

* You may begin to experience more social anxiety even around those closest to you.

* Your attention span is severely limited. Carrying on a conversation can be difficult.

* You may feel self-conscious being around others while you are feeling so off. Trying to act like *the old you* takes energy you may not have.

* You may experience sensory overload in public—more sensitive to large crowds and loud noises.

* You find small talk unbearable. Excruciating, in fact.

* You have less tolerance for gossip or anything petty.

* You may become more real with people; just saying it like it is.

* You may tear up easier and become more sentimental with those you care about when you see them.

* Your circle of friends may change as your interests change and you become a new you.

* It becomes easier to let go of unbalanced, draining relationships. This clarity means cutting certain toxic people out of your life *and it can feel freeing.*

* The process can feel like a metamorphosis.

In the beginning, you will feel very raw. This is natural.

Change or the unknown can feel very scary. Loss of this magnitude can be overwhelming in ways we just don't know how to process. Try to keep in mind:

* There is no end point, but the pain of grieving will soften with the passage of time.

* In time, you'll experience more good hours in the day than bad; then more better days than bad. That's how you know you're moving through it.

* You will grieve in some way for the rest of your life. It's natural. She was your *mom.*

* Grief changes you forever.

A mother's love is like no other love, naturally her loss is like no other loss. Try to be patient with the process and with yourself.

CHAPTER 4

How Long Will This Pain Last?

There's no clear-cut timeline for grief and everyone's process is different. A person's emotional makeup, the circumstances surrounding the death, the relationship with your mother, your support system, and your natural coping mechanisms all factor in.

Some people may feel better after a few weeks or months, and for others, it may take years. The grief process is slippery—in the midst of recovering there may be falls and setbacks. For that reason, it's essential to treat yourself with compassion as you allow the process to unfold.

All this is unpredictable and unique to the person going through it.

Throughout the healing process, grief will vary in its intensity. Give yourself time to experience the ebb and flow of emotions. Try to just go with every bump without judgement, knowing it's all moving you forward and through it.

IT'S DIFFERENT FOR EVERYONE

I was unmarried, not in a significant relationship, and had no children. My mother was loving and so full of life. She was always my biggest cheerleader and best source of unconditional love.

Her death was sudden and unexpected.

I'm very independent, but I didn't realize how much my mom was my center of gravity until she died. She had such a large presence in life; it's no wonder why her absence left such a large void. I had to learn to become my own center once she was gone.

Everyone's story is different. Everyone's process is different.

THE FIRST 90 DAYS

For most people, and for obvious reasons, dealing with your mother's loss is hardest at the beginning.

In the first three months, you cry a lot, if not every day. Anything can trigger your emotions and you may not have the energy to do the most basic things like getting out of bed, eating, cooking, running errands, and going to work.

You may find that crying in the shower now becomes a daily ritual.

In the first few weeks, there is the funeral or service to get through. During this time, it may be hard to be around other people. You may just want to pull the shades, stay in bed, and crumble. That's okay.

Letting yourself cry and cocoon for a while is perfectly natural. In fact, it's enormously healing. It releases and soothes a lot of pent-up, incredibly sad energy.

I think it's absolutely nuts that many employers only give three days paid time off for bereavement leave, and a more "generous" policy might include up to five days off.

No one can process grief in 3-5 days. Please don't put that expectation on yourself.

In the first few months, you are just settling into the reality that your mom is gone. You've now made it through the whirlwind of the days following her death and her funeral, but the cards and calls start to fade.

In the quiet, loneliness and grief really begin to find their way in.

I don't think most people realize the amount of grieving that continues long after the rest of the world "goes on." That's when you may really need a little extra support.

If you do need anything, it's important to ask for help. Most people are uncomfortable with grief. The fact they may say nothing doesn't mean they don't care. It usually means they don't know how to help or what to do.

Reach out if you need something. The ones who care about you will be glad you did.

In the first few months, try not to push yourself too soon to make any important decisions or rush to clean out her personal things.

Going through your mother's personal belongings, especially, is a deeply emotional, sometimes overwhelming experience that you want to take your time with.

You can always box items for later if you have to clear things out, but give yourself room to decide what to keep in the family, what to pass on to her other loved ones, or what to give to charity once your mind is less foggy and you're breathing normally again.

It's a horrible feeling to make a hurried decision and part with something of hers that you cannot get back.

FROM 3 TO 6 MONTHS

Things become a little easier, the pain less stabbing and you may find more moments of peace.

You'll remember when you laugh for the first time again. You may feel a little guilty when you do. "I shouldn't be happy. My mom is dead." Boy, is that a common feeling.

It could be months before you find moments of happiness, but you will get there.

On the outside, you may look normal again, but on the inside, you're still working through a lot of emotions and have a way to go.

6 MONTHS TO A YEAR

Each month of the first year is ticked off the calendar like a minor achievement. You'll note that you've made it through another 30 days!

As you make it through all the "firsts" without your mom—birthdays, holidays, anniversaries, special occasions—the sadness is revisited again each time.

There is a lot to adjust to. As you move through the days and months of the first year, you feel where she is missing from your life over and over again.

Do you see why you need to allow yourself to go easy? The wound starts to heal and then the scab gets picked at again and again during that first year.

The First Year & Beyond

You may find some relief as the second year rolls around. As you become more aware of how different things are, it can still hurt but not as deeply as that first year. Now you're prepared.

Still, others have found that the second year is harder as the weight of reality really settles in. Everyone is different.

Most people going through grief agree that it takes a full year or two, and sometimes more, just to start to feel somewhat normal again.

Long-Term Adjustment

After two years and beyond, I still experience days where the sadness hits out of nowhere. It's always there just below the surface still.

Those moments may come up for the rest of our lives, but the depth of the pain you feel in the beginning won't be so profound. The hurt will fade, but memories of her won't.

As you work through everything you'll find your love for your mother is as strong as ever, but her loss changes you and your life in some ways forever.

THE NEW NORMAL

I don't think I've ever met anyone who ever truly gets over a loss like this. You adjust.

In time, hopefully, you create a new normal—a term you'll hear often in the grief recovery world to describe life after loss.

In time, you find a new you and a new life structure without the physical presence of your mother.

CHAPTER 5

Your Mother's Presence

In the beginning, talking about your mom may be all you want to do. You barely notice there's a world outside your grief.

Why does talking about your mom feel so good? Because it keeps her alive. Because it brings her to you in the present moment. Because others are able to get to know her better. Because in sharing, people get to know you better and more deeply understand what you've lost. Because she *IS* so much of who you *are*. Because you love her and it's healing.

Listening to stories about your mother and hearing her name spoken can also feel good. Encourage people to share. Memories about her are like teddy bears for the heart.

Present Tense

Try to use the present tense when people ask you what your mother's name *was*. Let others know that your mother remains present in your life and that all references to her are in the present as well.

"My mother's name *is* _____," tell them. She still has a name and it feels empowering to use it. Her name doesn't die with her. Do you feel the difference?

Poor Example 1: "My mother's name *was* Irma." In the past tense, it feels final. Like it's all over.

Good Example 2: "My mother's name *is* Irma." That's it! Her name remains. Her essence remains. Who she was to you remains. Her life mattered.

She still *is* your mother. I also remind myself: I *am* still her daughter.

KEEPING YOUR RELATIONSHIP ALIVE

Another way I keep my mom present is to talk to her in my head, whether it's on a walk, while cooking or just commenting about something throughout the day.

Recently, I found a movie theater gift card that she had given me. My mom loved the movies. I rarely go, but when I would, it was usually with her during one of her visits and we'd make a fun day of it: Mani-pedis, lunch, a movie.

I haven't been in some time, so I decided to go and thought to myself, "Come on Mom, let's go see a show. It's on me!" I could hear her laugh (oh, that laugh) and say, "*On you?* This is on me—I gave you that card!"

It was her voice and humor.

Some members of our bereavement support group, *Healing After the Loss of Your Mother – Grief Support* (an online Facebook group I formed in July 2016), have shared how good it feels to journal to their mothers, writing out all the news, gossip, and events of the day just like they would when she was alive.

Another member shared, "When I need her, I ask my mom what to do and then wait for the answer. I let her mother me still. I knew what she said to me in the past when I was hurting and it comforted me back then, so why not now? That part of her that loved me so much continues to help me. Our love was real and it endures."

There are so many ways we can continue to feel our mothers presence in our lives and keep that relationship alive. Our love and connection doesn't leave us. It just changes forms.

FILLING THE EMOTIONAL VOID

Grief involves a lot more than just missing someone. On a physical level, we grieve our mother's loss.

On an emotional level, we grieve the loss of who she was, the role she played and how she made us feel: loved, nurtured, protected, special.

Your mother held that space for you.

When she's gone, you feel the void.

But in time, you may begin to build the qualities of who she was inside yourself. A part of healing is learning to step into the space that is left.

If you had a strong mother who could put a bully in their place, you might find yourself becoming more assertive in her absence. She was sponsoring the energy of "protector" for you while she was alive.

Or in the absence of a nurturing mother, you might learn to gently mother yourself like she did.

When you begin to merge some of her qualities inside yourself, you might recognize how much she *is* a part of who you *are*.

She continues to have a living presence as you begin to nurture and love yourself.

CHAPTER 6

Grief Work vs. Allowing

I really dislike the term "grief work." Maybe it's because I didn't want one more obligation or pressure hanging over me. The reality is, grief happens whether you work with it or not.

Healing shouldn't be an added burden. It's sometimes easier just think of it as *allowing a natural process to unfold.*

Call it organic healing.

SURRENDER

Grief is really about surrender. It's about being brave enough to be vulnerable.

As you begin processing your grief, you will recognize that your feelings are natural. Go with them. Surrender to them.

Grief just isn't something you can fight or rationalize away. As you talk to others going through loss, you'll see your reactions are very common and you just need to ride through some uncomfortable times.

The waves get smaller in time, and you learn how to navigate them.

For me, I looked at it like an emotional riptide. The more you fight it, the harder it is. If you go with the (emotional) currents, you are eventually taken safely to shore.

RELEASING

In "A New Earth: Awakening Your Life's Purpose," spiritual teacher Eckhart Tolle writes, "Any negative emotion that is not fully faced and seen for what it is in the moment it arises does not completely dissolve. It leaves behind a remnant of pain."

This process is all about allowing uncomfortable feelings to be. We look at them, honor them, step back, and know they are temporary on their way to being released.

Just keep breathing, and then let it go.

THE FLOW OF THINGS

As you move through the grieving process, you will discover many thoughts about the stages and progression of grief. Is there a flow to it or do you really have to work it?

J. William Worden, a professor of psychology at Harvard Medical School, proposed a practical alternative to the stage-based models of mourning that rang true to me.

He divided the bereavement process into the Four Tasks of Mourning. They aren't really "tasks" per se; grief does most of the work. You just move with it:

1. Accept the reality of the loss.
2. Work through the pain of grief.
3. Adjust to life without the deceased.
4. Maintain a connection to the deceased while moving forward with life.

That is a fairly simple and straightforward model, and what one can generally expect to experience as they make their way through grief. Everyone's progression, however, will be unique to them.

As you move through your own process, you may jump around between emotions and general steps. However it comes, just try to allow, allow, allow.

In your journey through grief, healing happens.

CHAPTER 7

Grief Triggers

Part of grieving will include grief triggers. Be aware—they are those unexpected memories that bring up the pain of loss all over again.

They are stealth and hit you out of the blue.

You might be happily cooking dinner, then your mom's favorite song comes on and, "Bam!", you are in tears all over again.

These triggers are moments of reawakened grief. They can happen anytime, anywhere.

Grief triggers are especially strong in the beginning when you don't know what might "get" you and when your emotions are right at the surface.

The trigger can be anything big or small. It can be coming across something with her handwriting on it; the smell of her perfume; her favorite holiday; eating her favorite dish; passing her favorite restaurant chain; seeing her favorite flower; hearing the sound of an emergency vehicle; attending a memorial service; watching her favorite movie or series come on TV; hearing someone who laughs like her; the sound of wind chimes that she loved so much...

They can make you tear up or get a lump in your throat, or send you into an unstoppable bawling episode.

The effects of a trigger can last for minutes or linger for days. Like grief itself, they are unpredictable.

When these moments do arise, try to recognize what you are feeling, acknowledge it, and let it move through your heart and body.

In time, grief triggers lose their potency. In time, you can know what yours are and what to expect. In time, you remember they are there because your mother was always in your heart... and always will be.

CHAPTER 8

Holidays and Special Occasions

Holidays, birthdays, anniversaries and special occasions are usually happy times of the year and involve some of our favorite childhood memories. After your mom is gone, they become our most dreaded.

Getting through the first year of special occasions is by far the hardest. They become reminders, again, that she's not here. You feel her loss again as each one comes around.

These special days are a big grief trigger for most people.

That's no surprise. Moms just have a way of making these times–*and us*–feel special. They just aren't the same without her touch and her presence.

PLAN AHEAD

Besides difficulty on the date itself, there also tends to be a lot of anxiety in the days leading up to each special day as grief resurfaces.

There is a lot of nervous anticipation. You don't know what to expect or how you'll feel.

Knowing special days may bring some emotional uncertainty, it's helpful to make a plan in advance for how you'd like to spend the day.

New Traditions

Decide if you want to stick with old traditions or build new ones. You may find that creating new traditions lets you look forward to a new way of doing things—ways that don't carry memories of the past or have the sting of sadness attached to them.

It's also perfectly reasonable to pass on any special day you're just not feeling up to. See how you feel. Play by ear.

There's no need to burden yourself doing anything that doesn't feel comfortable. If you are feeling raw, anxious or overwhelmed, it's okay. Tell your family and friends how you are feeling and that you might not be up for attending any events right now.

The Holiday Season

The holiday season is an especially hard time of year. It usually begins as early as September as the weather starts to change, leaves start turning color and seasonal decorations start going up in stores.

Instead of a joyful, anticipated time of year, this becomes a big red flag to those grieving. They know what's coming.

What's to celebrate when you know you're going to miss all the things your mother did to make the holidays so memorable?

If you don't feel like you can handle the holidays at any time, it's perfectly fine to have an alternate plan. Perhaps you take a vacation instead this year or go to the movies or just stay in bed and order take-out. Maybe you just skip it altogether and just make it a day like any other.

If you choose to attend a celebration, you can let people know in advance that you are having a hard time and may need to cut it short. Allow yourself some wiggle room.

There's so much stress around the holidays, anyway. You don't need to put added pressure on yourself.

To help minimize any holiday-related anxiety, you might also consider avoiding the malls and large crowds. Shop early in the day if you do need to get out, or buy your groceries a week in advance of a major holiday.

Also, ordering gifts online is a big help in avoiding the mad rush of shoppers and any potential triggers.

INTRODUCING NEW CUSTOMS

If you choose to attend traditional occasions, there are ways to enjoy them. One way is to introduce new customs that will honor and include your mother.

It may be through baking her favorite dessert, including her favorite meal, playing her favorite songs, lighting a remembrance candle or sharing favorite stories about her.

Of course, you will miss her, but you can always honor her and include her presence at a traditional gathering in new and heart-felt ways.

MOTHER'S DAY

Besides the holiday season, few things can sting more than your first Mother's Day without your mom.

I was prepared to feel sad on that day. I wasn't prepared for the many days of television commercials, Mother's Day cards, gift displays and commercialism in the stores leading up to it.

On the day of hearing someone say, "Happy Mother's Day," or "What are you doing for Mother's Day?" at the grocery store was too much. My eyes welled up with tears and all I wanted was to get out of there as fast as I could.

On any holiday, there are so many emotional potholes to be aware of. This one is, literally, the mother of all holidays.

If you don't quite know what to do, it can be nice to celebrate your mother in your own way. Consider doing something she enjoyed or some kind of gesture with her in mind. It doesn't have to be anything big or fancy.

Anytime you show your love for your mother in some way, it helps to continue to feel her in your heart. It doesn't need to be reserved for or done on any one day.

HER BIRTHDAY

Your mom's birthday can be especially hard because it is a day that was all about her. It was *her* special day.

I wasn't expecting this to hit me as hard as it did. You think about how old she'd be. What she'd be doing. How she would have liked to have celebrated the day.

If you feel sad that day, you have choices. You may decide to spend her birthday in quiet reflection. Many people who've just lost their mothers feel compelled to do something—no matter how big or small—as a nice way to continue the celebration of her life. It is possible to bring some joy to the day.

Oftentimes, other family members and friends are anticipating the day and wondering what to do, as well. Some find great comfort in gathering together and, for example, going to her favorite restaurant; baking her favorite birthday cake together or sharing happy stories.

It's a good feeling when you can see how your mom can still bring you all together.

If you're looking for a more private way to acknowledge the day, you can also volunteer at her favorite charity or do an activity she loved. Perhaps plant a tree or garden, something you can watch flourish and visit again as it grows.

Your love for your mother doesn't stop. There's no reason the celebration of her and the connection you feel should either.

YOUR BIRTHDAY

Your birthday can be tough because no one seems to make you feel as special on your day like the woman who gave birth to you—whether you were born through her body or from her heart.

Your mother probably had special things she did for you every year: The cards, the phone call or text, all the little things she'd do to make you feel celebrated. It just seems a little empty when she's gone and those things stop coming.

In the beginning, it's common to lose that "happy" birthday feeling without her. And you know what? It's okay to feel sad.

I didn't want to acknowledge my birthday that first year. By the second, I didn't want to feel bad again and decided to make my birthday more about my mom and appreciate the fact she gave me life. I tried to make it a reminder of the joy she always felt on that day.

Each year forward usually gets a little easier. Happy memories do have a way of finding their way back into your mind.

THE ANNIVERSARY OF HER DEATH

The anniversary of her death is naturally difficult. It brings up everything you've lost all over again. It also feels like an important milestone in recognizing all you've come through in a year.

I was anxious about how to deal with the first anniversary date. My friend suggested doing what I needed for myself that day if anything, and not feel forced to acknowledge it in any particular way.

Always remember: there's no right way to do any of this. There's only your way.

She said, "If it's too much to handle, it's all right to look at the anniversary of her death as just another day without her. You don't need to make it special."

Just the first year, I wanted to do something. I chose to plant a tree in my backyard. I call it my hugging tree and it makes me feel good to watch it grow. Plus, my mom loved her garden so much. It felt like a comforting way to pay tribute to her and think about her in a good way every day, not just one day of the year.

MAKING THINGS YOUR OWN

It's not easy to experience so much change and make so many adjustments that first year. In time, creating new traditions—or blending new customs together with old traditions—can help you move forward and keeps your mother present in new ways on special days.

My mom is so much a part of my heart. When I bring something into my home or a holiday that reminds me of her, I feel her with me. I think of her with love and feel she is still a part of my life this way.

Yes, there is sadness, but her essence and the memory of her can always be included.

CHAPTER 9

Coping Tools & Strategies

*"Strength of character isn't always about how much
you can handle before you break,
it's also about how much you can handle
after you've been broken."*

— Unknown

As you process your grief, you'll first feel like a complete mess.

As the days go by and you start to feel stronger, you'll want to find ways to nourish yourself and restore a little balance back into your life.

I found that the better I began to feel physically, the better I started to feel emotionally. Grief hits on every level—mentally, physically and spiritually—so taking a three-pronged approach to healing is something that I found helpful.

You nurture each part of you. It's a healthy habit of self-care and one you can build on.

At first, I found it really helps to establish a new daily routine that I could look forward to. When so much of your life is out of control, some structure and moments of daily consistency can help keep you moving forward in a positive way. It grounds and centers you.

There are many constructive ways to help balance out the negative feelings you may have—consider these your toolbox of support for the mind, body, and soul.

MIND

What you focus on is a choice. It's not always an easy one, but it is yours. If it feels like grief is running the show, try these helpful tips:

* **"Honor. Feel. Heal."**

If in the beginning, all you can do is remember these three words, start there. Try to:

> **Honor** whatever feelings come up.
> **Feel** your feelings, even the unpleasant ones. They are coming up to be acknowledged and released.
> **Heal.** That's the outcome we are trying to reach, and we get there in baby steps.

* **Gentle Self-Talk**

Soothing self-talk is really important. Keep reminding your-self you're doing the best you can. You will have good days and bad. Forgive yourself if you don't know how to "get it right." *There is no right.* It may be temporarily chaotic, and that's to be expected.

Hopefully, you wouldn't put up with a negative friend talking to you with judgment. Please don't do it to yourself.

Be your own best supportive friend with your thoughts.

❋ The Value of Crying

Hands down, there's nothing that provides more relief than a good, deep cry. Pretending you're okay takes so much energy—energy you probably don't have right now.

Judith Orloff, MD, a psychiatrist and best-selling author of *Emotion Freedom: Liberate Yourself from Negative Emotions and Transform Your Life* has witnessed "the healing power of tears" in her role as a physician for over twenty years.

In an article by Dr. Orloff in Psychology Today (July 2010) she describes how tears are the body's release valve for stress, sadness, grief, anxiety, and frustration. Tears are cleansing.

She writes, "To stay healthy and release stress, I encourage my patients to cry. For both men and women, tears are a sign of cour-age, strength, and authenticity."

Tears are usually just below the surface when you're grieving, but you may worry that if you start, you might not be able to stop. If you're depressed, you're holding back.

I have a friend with a very busy life, but she allowed herself a 10-minute "cry time" whenever she needed it. It helped.

The release of tears feels like a giant emotional exhale from the body. It helps you move through your pain and closer to healing.

❋ Getting It Out

If you feel self-conscious about a good, hard release cry because you may have others in your home—or when crying into a pillow isn't enough—your car can become its own sacred space.

You can cry, yell, and get out pent up, really intense feelings and no one is there to hear or judge you. Just don't park in front of your nosy neighbor's house.

I, like many in grief, would get into my car and scream if I had to, bawl, pound on the steering wheel if parked, and just let it all out.

Another method of release I came up with is "swear therapy." It helped when anger was the emotion of the moment. First, get in your car. Next, pick your favorite swear word. Then, scream it for a good 10 seconds as loud as you can. Repeat as needed.

I found it very freeing. I truly *swear* by it.

❋ Writing & Journaling

You can write feelings out so they don't stay trapped inside. There are some thoughts and feelings you would never repeat to another person. Writing becomes a safe outlet and your journal a most trusted, non-judgmental friend.

Expressive writing is a path to healing. Dr. James Pennebaker, author of *Writing to Heal: A Guided Journal for Recovering from*

Traumatic and Emotional Upheaval explains that stress often comes from emotional blockages. He writes, "When we translate an experience into language, we essentially make the experience graspable." The result is freeing yourself from the mental grip of emotional difficulties or trauma.

Your writing can be stream of consciousness; it doesn't have to be structured. This also helps you see how far you've come as you look back on the pages if you are so inclined.

Writing helps clear your mind and release pent-up feelings. It moves emotional energy in your body and provides a beneficial release.

❋ Point or Pivot

It's important to give yourself permission to feel whatever you are feeling, both good and bad. Sometimes, however, it can feel like you're stuck in emotional quicksand with compulsive or negative thought patterns.

I once attended a seminar by intuitive guide Karen Hager and psychologist and astrologer Michael Lennox about developing a spiritual practice.

One very helpful tool they talked about was consciously pointing your feelings in the direction you want to go.

Think of it as "Point or Pivot."

> **Point:** If a thought feels good or positive, point in that direction and keep going.
>
> **Pivot**: If a thought feels bad or negative, stop. Pivot. Head towards the other direction. Change your stream of thoughts.

This is a basic principle behind The Law of Attraction; you get what you think about.

I feel uplifted watching YouTube videos of Esther Hicks talking about The Law of Attraction and the Teachings of Abraham. On this subject she has said, "Keep reaching for the feeling of relief. That becomes your point of attraction."

It's a simple principle to apply and easy to use once you are aware of your thoughts.

✴ Gratitude Journal

When you're overcome with sadness, it can be hard to see what is going right in your life.

A gratitude journal—the simple act of writing down things that you have to be thankful for—can help shift your perspective and focus.

Getting into this habit can be a powerful tool in helping bring awareness about the good things in your life, no matter how simple.

Things to be grateful for are there if you look for them.

They can be something as simple as the love of an animal, the nice weather, a flower in bloom, the sun rising another day, a beautiful sunset, a good meal or someone's kind gesture.

Try writing down three things you were grateful for that day. An attitude of gratitude may be a habit that takes time to grow.

When you do begin, you'll gain a new awareness that builds upon itself.

While there are times you need to address your pain head-on in healthy ways, there are also times where you just need a break.

As you put yourself back together, try to introduce a little joy into your world. Treat your mind in other ways and learn to engage with life again. Some mind-related and mood-boosting suggestions:

* **Take A Vacation From Grief**

Grief can feel exhausting and all-consuming. Give yourself some relief by taking your mind off of things for a while. Keep things light.

Go to a movie, a concert or the theatre; enjoy a spectator sport; stroll through an art gallery; go to a park and play on the swings like you did when you were a kid; put your feet in the sand; get a massage; treat yourself to a manicure; read a good book; go for a drive, and find someplace new.

Find a new adventure and give your busy mind a vacation.

* **Creativity**

Art, painting, scrapbooking, gardening, anything that lets you express your inner world outwardly is a great way to keep emotions from feeling trapped. Tapping into your creativity takes your mind out of grief and closer to the natural joy inside.

* **Funny Movies or Videos**

Watch anything that helps lighten your mood. Old sitcoms, funny movies, blooper reels, etc.

An easy mood booster can be going to YouTube and watching cute animal videos. Nothing beats the joy of jumping baby pigmy goats in pajamas to lift your mood!

Have you seen "Simon's Cat," the animated short series on YouTube? Hilarious. Seek out the things that elevate and lighten your outlook. Allow yourself to laugh again.

❀ Sound Healing

Sound has been used by many cultures for thousands of years for healing. Its goal is to move you from a place of unbalance to a place of balance through the healing vibration of sound.

Sound healing is a passive experience as you lay down, breathe deeply, and let the soothing, vibrational sounds of gongs, Tibetan singing bowls, sounds of nature or binaural beats wash over you.

It helps to relax your whole body, slow your breathing and soothe your emotions.

❀ Touchstones

I keep words of inspiration around my home to whisper over the busy mind. They are positive messages that reach below conscious awareness… and it works!

I write words like peace, love, tranquility, courage on rocks with a marker pen; buy shells with encouraging words on them or pictures with positive messages.

For me, these touchstones are gentle reminders that promote a sense of encouragement and balance.

♦   **Music**

Free your mind. Upbeat music is connected to the pleasure center in the brain.

Listening to it can have an immediate, positive impact on our emotions. Happy, upbeat music is a mood booster, increases energy and reduces feelings of stress.

BODY

Bereavement does take a toll on the body. These tips are offered to help you stay balanced on a physical level:

* **Sleeping**

Some days are just too overwhelming. Listen to your body. If it's telling you it needs sleep or if you just want to pull the covers over your head, then go back to bed.

Go to sleep. It's okay. You can try again tomorrow.

* **Good Nutrition**

Comfort foods can help make you feel emotionally better, but often it tends to be heavy, fried, processed, and lacks nutritional value. Too much can make you lethargic or add to depressive feelings. Still, they have their place when you need nostalgic soothing.

It's funny how the foods you crave tend to match where you are emotionally. Low mood = low vibrational, processed foods. Happier mood = lighter, higher vibrational foods with live energy (as opposed to processed) like fruits and vegetables.

High vibrational, healthy food will keep your body feeling lighter and help improve your overall energy and outlook.

Also, try to limit or avoid putting stimulants such as caffeine, alcohol, and sugar into your already sensitive system right now.

* **Deep Breathing**

When we're stressed or in grief, our breaths tend to be shallow.

Deep belly breathing can boost your energy, reduces stress, and improves heart health. It also helps release anxiety and alleviates stress and depression.

Rebecca Dennis, a breath coach and author of *And Breathe: The Complete Guide to Conscious Breathing*, explains that deep breathing heals on many levels and is important for our mental and physical well-being. It invigorates red blood cells and releases metabolic waste product.

"By breathing deeply, you allow the diaphragm to drop downward, the rib cage to expand and create more space for the lungs to inflate," she writes. "By mastering the art of deep breathing, increased oxygen floods into the body, eventually helping the heart pace to slow down to create feelings of calmness and relaxation."

If you find yourself stressed, take note of how you are breathing then go deep. Inhale calm. Exhale stress. Repeat.

❖ Exercise & Movement

When you're strong enough to get out of bed or off the couch, try moving your body. The more you do, the easier it will become, and the better you will feel.

Stretching, yoga, deep breathing, light exercise, getting to the gym, going for even a short walk will all benefit your body and mood.

You can start slowly, at least 15 minutes a few times a week, and build as you feel stronger.

Doing something physical like hitting a punching bag can also release a lot of tension—especially anger if that's an emotion you are struggling with.

Remember, emotions are energy and you don't want to keep them trapped in your body. Exercise helps move them.

* **Walks in Nature**

Walking has a way of clearing your head and getting your blood circulating. It literally keeps you moving forward.

I found connecting to Mother Nature very helpful and peaceful. It also helps keep you *present* as you ignore the busy world and just take in your surroundings.

While on a walk, if you've never hugged a tree, give it a try. They are strong and have energy. If you hug one, feel it hug you back. Try feeling Mother Earth's unconditional love.

* **Stay Hydrated**

It's sometimes hard to remember to eat, and it's really easy to forget the importance of drinking enough water and staying hydrated.

Your body depends on water to function. Every cell, tissue, and organ in your body needs water to work properly. If you don't get enough water, other grief symptoms like fatigue, headaches, confusion, lightheadedness can worsen.

No tears when crying? Doctors say it can be a sign of dehydration.

"In general, you should try to drink between half an ounce and an ounce of water for each pound you weigh, every day," advises Trent Nessler, PT, DPT, MPT, managing director of Baptist Sports Medicine in Nashville in an WebMD article on water and your diet (published July 7, 2010.)

For example, a 140-pound person = 70 ounces of water a day.

Soul

When you're in the thick of it, it's sometimes hard to remember: You are not your grief. Coming back to your center can be made easier when you implement activities that focus on your heart, soul, and balance, such as:

* **Grounding**

You've no doubt been feeling low on energy and unbalanced like you need to recharge your batteries.

Well, the earth is like a giant energy battery that provides a natural charge from the ground.

Grounding is a centering practice that connects you energetically to the earth. It allows you to be more fully in your body, in the present moment, while receiving nourishing energy from the earth. It helps balance your physical and spiritual bodies.

To do this, try the following:

1. Go barefoot.
2. Put your feet in the grass or on the earth. Wiggle your toes.
3. Imagine roots going from the soles of your feet down deep into the core of the earth. Imagine that energy coming back up into you.
4. Breathe deeply.

Be fully in your body. Clear your mind and be completely in the moment. Feel the energy of the earth. Learn to be still.

❋ Nurture Yourself

Tend to your mind, body, and soul as you seek comfort. Take a warm bath. Cook yourself something nutritious and tasty. Wrap yourself in a comfy blanket and soft socks.

Treat yourself like you would do a dear friend or loved one. Be compassionate, gentle, and forgiving.

When your mom's not there, remember to mother yourself.

❋ Meditation

Meditation helps the mind to be quiet and is important for life balance.

Even if you can only do it for a few minutes at a time, it can help bring in a small sense of peace. It may feel slow at first when your focus is off, but with practice, you can build on it.

Group meditations may also be worth trying. In doing so, it gets you out of the house and in the company of others, without having to talk about what you're going through.

When concentrating in your own mind is just too difficult, try guided meditations. YouTube is a great resource for finding topics that may resonate with you. Simply type in "guided meditations" as a subject matter that interests you: Grief, calm, self-love, anger, anxiety, inner peace, insomnia, etc.

After learning about it in our grief support group, I tried guided Yoga Nidra meditation (yogic sleep as it is commonly known) and found it very helpful. It's a powerful relaxation and meditation technique that is easy to follow and is incredibly soothing.

Yoga Nidra allows the body to restore and balance itself. As you lay down, it simply guides you to a deep state of relaxation that promotes inner peace, calm and deep rest.

It's an especially helpful tool if you are having trouble falling asleep and staying there.

✦ Prayer

"Prayer is when you talk to God; Meditation is when you listen to God." – Diane Robinson

Whoever your source of power is, talk to them. Even if you only talk to nature or your dog, you are connecting with unconditional love and that is healing.

✦ Connection / Community

We tend to isolate ourselves when we are grieving. You may also be sensitive to overstimulation right now and not in a mood to talk.

When alone starts to feel lonely, a little community helps. There are still ways to get social interaction without exhausting yourself.

Try activities that involve other people but don't require too much social energy like yoga, group meditation, kickboxing or aerobics, hitting the gym, painting lessons, strolling through an art gallery, going to church, or attending a spiritual seminar.

You don't need to say a word to feel the company of others. This can be a nice, easy way to transition back into the outside world.

CHAPTER 10

The Emotional Pain Scale

Like a physical pain scale used in hospitals, I started using an "Emotional Pain Scale" to track where I was on any given day. I think you'll find it useful.

1 was no pain. 10 was intense pain.

At the beginning, I found the pain scale as an easy shorthand when people close to me wanted to gauge my emotional state of well-being.

"How are you doing today?" they'd ask. "Meh," I'd reply. "About a 6."

In those early days, my emotions were all over the place.

I might start at a 9, go to a 4, and end up at a 7. This actually helped me identify what made me feel better, and what dragged my emotions lower. I wrote it all down.

I just wanted to feel better, so this became a very helpful tracking tool.

You may be surprised at how you can help shift your mood when you are more aware of your feelings and what affects them.

It also helps to see the overall progress made as the weeks go by.

THE PAIN *WILL* LESSEN IN TIME

I know it's probably difficult to believe right now, but people who have gone through grief and loss swear it won't hurt with this ferocity forever. They promise. I promise. Keep reminding yourself of that.

The common phrase: "There's no way around grief, only through it" is true. Just know it *will* get better... and then keep on going.

CHAPTER 11

Grief vs. Depression

As you grieve, you may wonder: "Is this depression or grieving? Do I need medication?"

I'm not a medical professional. My personal experience was this: In the first few days following my mom's death, the surge of emotions overloaded my mind and body; my heart was racing and my blood pressure so dangerously high that I wound up in the emergency room. Twice.

The substantial emotional and physical impact on my body wasn't something I could personally just pray or meditate away. I needed help.

My doctor prescribed an anti-anxiety medication, but I knew it would only be a very short-term fix. I'd eventually need to work through this myself.

In the heavy weeks that followed, however, I wondered if I needed some longer-term help for my depression, so I sought out different kinds of therapy and doctors.

I found that conventional Western medicine, in general, is more apt to treat the symptoms of grief with anti-anxiety drugs and anti-depressants.

Many do find that traditional therapy and medication are very helpful when they experience symptoms of clinical depression— or when, for example, even the most simple day-to-day routines seem overwhelming even after a period of time.

The struggle is real.

I tried a few holistic practitioners, as well. They didn't treat me or my symptoms with prescription drugs – they saw my grief in the early weeks as a natural state to process and experience. One told me, "You're not depressed. You're grieving." I was told I'd feel depressed while in grief, but that the two are different.

If at any time you are concerned about how you are about prolonged or complicated grief that isn't improving with time or any underlying issues that are persisting, please consult your physician, grief counselor or mental health practitioner to determine what's best for you, your mind and your body.

They are there to help, wherever you are in the grief journey.

In the meantime, how do you tell the difference between grief and depression when symptoms mimic each other?

Grief is not a disease or mental disorder; it's a natural response to a significant loss. There's no magic pill to cure grief and nothing to run away from. You just need to go through it.

Depression is a clinical disorder that is different from normal grief. The feelings of sadness may be more constant and according to the National Institute of Mental Health (www.nimh.nih.gov), it can be treated with medications, psychotherapy, or a combination of the two.

The Mayo Clinic's website (www.MayoClinic.org) further explains, "Most people experiencing normal grief and bereavement have a period of sorrow, numbness, and even guilt and anger. Gradually these feelings ease, and it's possible to accept the loss and move forward."

As crazy as it sounds, depression actually serves an important role in the grieving process.

In the book *On Grief & Grieving*, Elisabeth Kubler-Ross and David Kessler describe the process of grief and the beneficial role depression plays.

The book explains how normal feelings of depression that come with grief are seen by our society as something that needs fixing. "Of course clinical depression that is left untreated, can lead to a worsening of one's mental state. But in grief, depression is a way for nature to keep us protected by shutting down the nervous system so we can adapt to something we feel we cannot handle."

Feeling depressed is there to help us. It isn't something we can—or should—just snap out of. It's a period to go through as you process grief. Sit with it. Experience it. Feel all the unpleasant emotions that come up.

According to Kubler-Ross and Kessler, "When you allow yourself to experience depression, it will leave as soon as it has served its purpose in your loss. As you grow stronger, it may return from time to time, but that is how grief works."

Depression, however uncomfortable, is just a stop on the way to healing.

COMPLICATED GRIEF

Sadness and intense grief are considered normal after we lose someone we love until we process and adapt to the loss. However, other factors can sometimes affect—and slow down—the grieving process.

"For some people, feelings of loss are debilitating and don't improve even after time passes. This is known as complicated grief, sometimes called persistent complex bereavement disorder," the Mayo Clinic explains. "In complicated grief, painful emotions are so long lasting and severe that you have trouble recovering from the loss and resuming your own life."

Complicated grief (CG) has been described as an ongoing, heightened state of mourning that keeps you from healing.

"Coping with Complicated Grief," an article featured in the Harvard Medical School's Harvard Health newsletter (published: December 2011), explains some factors that may put the griever at risk for this:

"Complicated grief is more likely to occur after a death that is traumatic — premature, violent, or unexpected. But in some people, even normal bereavement can produce complicated grief."

The article goes on to say: "Whether that happens depends on how a person copes, not just with trauma, but with loss. Everyone experiences unfulfilled hopes, broken romances, illness, and injury. For anyone who could not respond to earlier losses without losing emotional equilibrium, complicated grief becomes a greater danger. So a person with a history of depression, anxiety disorders, or a personality disorder is more likely to suffer complicated grief after bereavement, as well as PTSD if the loss was traumatic."

"The Nature of Complicated Grief," an article by researcher John Wilson, explains some factors that may put a person at higher risk for developing this:

* If it involves a violent death.

* If the death was sudden or unexpected.

* When there are issues related to how the person grieving was notified about the death.

* If they found or identified the body.

* Low family or social support.

* High dependency between the decedent in life.

* If the one grieving is prone to depression or neuroticism.

* Being young.

* Female.

* Age of your mother at her time of death.

• Problematic relationship with the deceased.

• Anxious, avoidant or insecure attachment style.

The Harvard Health newsletter suggests, "While it is hardly necessary for everyone who is grieving to seek professional help, people who develop complicated grief may need treatment."

SUICIDAL THOUGHTS

Fleeting suicidal thoughts are scary when you are grieving deeply, but grief experts say they are not uncommon and they usually pass.

I often hear people in bereavement support groups share that they don't want to live in a world without their mothers or they just want to be with her. In most cases, it's not that they truly want to die, but they just want relief from the pain.

Marty Tousley, RN, MS, FT, BC-FT and a registered nurse with a masters degree in Advanced Psychiatric-Mental Health Nursing, a nationally certified bereavement counselor and author of several books and articles on loss and grief, writes on her *Grief Healing* blog: "I can assure you that thoughts of suicide are not at all unusual when you are grieving."

She explains that "feeling a compelling need to end this agony of grief is completely understandable. Remember, though, that there is a vast difference between thinking about suicide and actually acting upon such thoughts. In grief, thoughts of suicide are usually fleeting and often reflect how desperately you want the pain of loss to end."

Emotions will fluctuate wildly as you grieve. The extreme pain you may feel at one moment may pass in the next. Such is the nature of the beast called grief.

If you are going through a dark period, gently remember two sayings: "This too shall pass" and "Suicide is a permanent solution to a temporary problem." Although they may sound trite, they are important to keep in mind.

If you are experiencing suicidal thoughts of any kind, please talk to someone.

During those dark times, it can be difficult to imagine ever getting out of it. If you reach out to others, you may find a lot of people who've been there, too.

Sometimes, simply vocalizing these feelings to another person who understands can help release those feelings.

Anytime these kinds of thoughts become more than just fleeting—in time or intensity--or you find yourself seriously thinking about harming yourself, please call 911 or The National Suicide Prevention Lifeline at 1-800-273-TALK (8255).

The National Suicide Prevention Lifeline provides free and confidential emotional support to people in suicidal crisis or emotional distress 24 hours a day, 7 days a week. They can also be found online at www.suicidepreventionlifeline.org.

If you are outside the United States, please visit the International Association for Suicide Prevention site at www.Iasp.info.

A doctor, mental health professional, or your place of worship can also be valuable, non-judgmental resources for help. Please reach out to someone.

WHEN TO SEEK HELP

I asked Lisa McGahey Veglahn, Vice President of Education, Hospice Foundation of America, how people might know that it may be time to seek professional help.

She said grief is often compared to a roller coaster ride with highs and lows that are pretty dramatic in the beginning, but will eventually level off.

She said if you find things aren't leveling off, then professional assistance can help.

WHERE TO FIND HELP

To find support, Veglahn suggests, "One good start might be with a hospice program in your area. Most hospices have grief groups or individual counseling, and it is available to anyone in the community," she said.

"(The individual) might also want to speak with (their) physician, but please be sure to share any grief reactions. While some medications may be helpful for some people, it is still important that the grief and loss is still addressed."

In addition to the Hospice Foundation of America (www.hospicefoundation.org), she also recommends, What's Your Grief at www.whatsyourgrief.com for other useful resources and helpful information.

THIS TAKES TIME

Going through this kind of grieving is anything but easy and is usually much bigger in more ways than any of us might have expected.

When I was feeling my lowest, I would think back on what my friend, Laura, told me: "You've already survived the worst day of your life so far, and that was the day your mom died. You will survive this."

You will, too.

Part II: How To Comfort Someone Who is Grieving

"Empathy is simply listening, holding space, withholding judgement, emotionally connecting, and communicating that incredibly healing message of 'You're not alone.'"

— Brené Brown

CHAPTER 12

The Supporter

You only lose your mother once.

Saying it's a monumental moment in a person's life doesn't even begin to describe how much it affects a person. Who is there for them when they go through it is something they remember for the rest of their life.

There may be some well-meaning people who want to help, but if they are not in touch with their own emotions, they can't be expected to be in touch with someone else's. They simply cannot give what they do not have.

Grief can also make people very uncomfortable. Some people just don't know what to do or say to someone in grief, so they just back away. Others just find it downright depressing.

Many may have a lot that they're dealing with in their own busy lives, and they just can't be there for another in a meaningful way.

Others may still be going through their own private pain, and this is too much for them to handle.

Just know, abandoning someone who has just lost one of the most important people in their life will feel to them like an added and hurtful loss if there's no explanation.

After feeling so raw and vulnerable, what they really need is gentle and solid support.

Understanding the Scope of Loss

Being tenderly present right now is key. Try to keep in mind the person grieving has lost so much more than just one of the most important people in their life.

They've lost the person they've probably loved the longest in their lifetime. They've lost a sense of security in the world. They've lost what others may take for granted, like just picking up the phone to chat. They've lost sharing everyday triumphs and heartaches with their mother. Holidays will be forever changed. Family dynamics are often affected. They've lost a lifetime of memories to come with that person.

Their world is changed forever.

As well-meaning as the words, "I'm sorry for your loss," may be, it just does not begin to acknowledge the magnitude of what else dies when someone loses their mother.

That's why your presence and holistic understanding is so important.

Your Role

If you're a friend or companion, your role as a supporter is to ride with the one in grief as a passenger beside them. Let them drive and just make sure they don't go off the road and over a cliff.

If you want to help, but you don't know how, here are some tips to keep in mind:

STEP ONE

Get familiar with Part I of this book: *For Those Who Are Grieving.* It's important to understand what your loved one is going through and what they may be feeling.

I thought I understood loss before, but I see now that I really had no idea about the profundity of what people who lose their mothers endure.

Don't feel bad if you don't know better. We can't show empathy or really be helpful if we don't understand the process. In our society today, we're simply not taught how to do this.

Once you get familiar with what emotions and stages your loved one might experience, you can offer more compassion. You'll also be better prepared for what to do when they hit those bumps in the road.

BE THE DEFINITION OF COMPASSION

To truly help someone in mourning, it helps to be walking examples of compassion and empathy.

What do those words *really* mean? Merriam-Webster defines them this way:

Compassion: Sympathetic consciousness of other's distress together with a desire to alleviate it.

Empathy: The feeling that you understand and share another person's experience and emotions: the ability to share someone else's feelings.

You don't need to fully understand, relate, or agree with another person's feelings to be a part of their healing. You simply need the desire to help and comfort them by listening to what they are going through.

By being there with love and without judgement, you help them feel less alone.

THE GIFT OF EMPATHY

Empathy is a gift if it's part of your nature and a gift when you offer it to another.

It's the ability to really relate by stepping into someone else's shoes.

SYMPATHY

Empathy is feeling *with* another, while sympathy is feeling compassion, sorrow or pity *for* the other person's hardship.

People grieving don't need your sympathy as much as they need your empathy.

HOLDING SPACE

How do you "hold space" for someone? It means you walk alongside them in their grief; let them feel their feelings without making them feel inadequate or trying to fix anything.

When you "hold space" for another, you open your heart with unconditional support, without judgement, and with love.

There is a powerful healing that comes when someone is given room to completely fall apart and know someone who cares will be there to help pick them back up.

This sacred zone is where they can feel whatever they need to feel to soften and release their pain.

GRIEF IS NOT A CONTEST

The person grieving is raw right now. Their focus is way off and they are typically overwhelmed.

Some well-meaning supporters may feel sharing the detailed story of their own loss is a way to relate, but it's not. Not now.

It can leave the one grieving feeling as if their experience is being minimized in some way. People in deep grief aren't capable of being the best listeners when their mind is this foggy. They're just trying to figure out how to survive this.

Try to remember that it's not a contest about whose experience was the most tragic or painful. Keep the focus on them. Share what's relatable, but don't shift focus.

This is about listening to *their* grief, *their* feelings, *and their* experience.

To Hug or Not to Hug

You would naturally think that a hug is the best thing you can offer to comfort someone when they are in pain and when words fail.

That's not necessarily true when it comes to grief.

"Please don't hug me. I'm in an emotional state and I will lose it," is what you may hear. Their fear: They are barely holding it together and are already on the verge of tears. A hug could burst the dam wide open.

Don't take it personally. When the person who is grieving gets stronger, hugs will be welcomed again.

Still, others in grief really need that physical embrace. When in doubt, just open your arms and ask before you hug.

CHAPTER 13

How To Help

You may feel awkward or unsure about how to comfort someone who is grieving. If that's the case, just gently ask them what they need.

Sometimes simply saying, "I don't know what to say or do, but I want you to know I care. I'm here for you," can be a great comfort.

The best kind of help you can offer can be broken down into three categories: Practical, physical, and emotional support.

PRACTICAL HELP

In the few first days and weeks after their mother's death, the one grieving is emotionally and physically exhausted. Doing the simplest tasks can feel overwhelming and things just don't get done.

Often, the bereaved may feel too uncomfortable to ask for—or accept—help. Many times, they don't even know what they need.

Rather than saying, "Let me know how I can help," offer specific assistance instead. Your assistance is, in all likelihood, desperately needed.

To show you care, be explicit. Ask if help is needed with such things as:

* Housework or hiring a maid to come over and clean.

* The laundry or going to the dry cleaner.

* Grocery shopping. (Stocking up on the food basics and also practical items like toilet paper, soap, etc.)

* Cooking or bringing over pre-cooked meals that are easy to serve. (Bring extra in small batches for the freezer.)

* Running any errands they may have.

* Watering their garden and plants or walking their dog.

* Offering to take over some regular duties like picking the kids up from school. Better yet, offer to take them out for play dates or excursions.

Other thoughtful touches you can do:

* Bring over easy to eat items, soups, and healthy snacks. The appetite of someone grieving is typically very low. Having convenient options makes it easier to put little nutrients in their body.

* Give them a gift card to their favorite restaurant. They don't usually want to cook for themselves for a while.

* If they have any favorite comfort foods take note and drop it off for them. It's like a hug from the inside.

* Bring cases of water. Make sure they're drinking plenty of it right now.

* They won't have the energy to do the dishes for a while. Bring over paper plates, napkins, and utensils.

* Fill up their car with gas and wash it.

* Bring them a box of thank you notes and stamps for any post-funeral correspondence.

* Drop off a basket of supplies for self-nurturing. Include things like lavender Epsom salt, white candles, spa music.

* Buy them extra handkerchiefs. Lots of them.

PHYSICAL COMFORT

Sometimes just having someone low-key present keeps the one who is grieving from feeling so alone. In the early days, I wanted to be alone but not lonely.

If you don't live with the person grieving, see if they want you to come over and cook for them. Do they want to go for a walk together? Talk? Go to a movie? Just sit on the couch and watch television without having to talk at all?

Ask them, "Do you want me to come over?" Or, if you live with them, see what kind of physical comfort or space they need.

Even if all they want to do is to be isolated right now, knowing that you're making yourself so available gives them a wonderful sense that you are truly there for them.

EMOTIONAL SUPPORT

There's nothing you can do to fix how fast someone who is mourning the loss of their mother will heal. That can be a powerless feeling for you as a supporter, but remember this is their journey.

To provide the most useful emotional support:

ᕲ Be present. Give them your full attention.

ᕲ Open your heart.

ᕲ Be an attentive listener. Let the one grieving talk, cry, ramble if they need to. This is the healthiest way they can process their grief.

ᕲ Be vulnerable. Cry if you need to. There's no shame in being authentic. It gives them permission to be the same.

ᕲ Validate their feelings.

👍 Don't interrupt. When they share, let them speak freely. They need to flow with whatever train of thought or feeling they feel.

👍 Tell them often: "Take your time."

👍 Let them know its okay to fall apart. They are safe with you.

👍 Don't put expectation or demands on them.

👍 Know their mother's name. Use it often.

👍 Ask about their mother. Get to know more about who she was. It is usually a comfort for them to talk about her. If it makes your loved one sad, they will tell you.

👍 Let them repeat the same stories if they need to. Don't edit them. It's part of their processing their emotional trauma.

👍 Ask them what their mom would do to make them feel comforted when they were little. Do those things when appropriate.

👍 Remember the date their mother died as well as her birthday. Do check in on those days.

👍 Be flexible. Their moods may change frequently. If they need to change plans or have problems committing, it's not that they're flaky; they're just trying to manage the emotional waves.

& Ask them how they are *today,* not the generic, "How are you?" This acknowledges that you recognize that overall it's a hard time and they are hurting. Ask how they are at this moment.

& Don't take things personally. Try to remember your loved one is processing a flood of emotions and they won't always make sense to you. (They won't make sense to the person grieving half the time either.)

& Be consistent. Check-in. Be there for the emotional long haul. (Support, in general, tends to taper off after the first few weeks or months. Be an exception, if you can.)

CHAPTER 14

What Not To Do

Now that you know *what to do* for someone in grief, it's important to be aware of *what not to do*. As the Dalai Lama wisely said, "Our prime purpose in this life is to help others. And if you can't help them, at least don't hurt them."

These are reminders of things to avoid doing:

✗ Don't judge. Everyone's process is their own.

✗ Don't try to fix them. They are not "broken," they are grieving.

✗ Don't put any pressure on them "to get over it." That would say more about your impatience than their effort to heal.

✗ Never use the words, "You're just..." It minimizes and invalidates the feelings they are expressing.

✗ Never use the word, "Should." Refrain from telling them what to do. There is no right or wrong in their journey, it's all theirs.

✗ Avoid using the words, "I know how you feel." No one can know exactly how another feels or how deep their pain is.

✗ Never point out the fact they may not be themselves right now. They are grieving deeply and pointing this out suggests they are doing something wrong.

✗ Don't give unsolicited advice.

✗ Don't try to control the conversation.

✗ If you have different religious or spiritual views, don't impose your values on them.

✗ Try not to hold temporary outbursts against them.

✗ Don't say, "You're so strong!" It gives an expectation that they should be, when in reality they may not be showing how truly "weak" they feel inside.

✗ Don't dry their tears as that stops their release of emotions. You can slide a tissue box to them, but let them cry so they let it out.

✗ Don't try to lighten the mood. The one grieving needs to feel whatever they need to feel.

✗ Words like "I'm worried about you" don't help. That puts the focus on your feelings and pressure on them to behave differently so you don't worry. Give them room to do what they need to do.

× Don't abandon them—emotionally or physically—when they're already feeling at their most vulnerable.

× Avoid saying things such as: "At least…" or "Your mother would want to see you happy." Your intention may be to cheer them up, but words won't help right now. Acknowledging their pain will.

× Avoid clichés ("Time heals all wounds;" "She's in a better place;" "Everything happens for a reason," etc.). They are hollow and hurtful. There is no silver lining in losing your mother.

Remember, grief isn't something that can be fixed. It's something that must be processed.

CHAPTER 15

Practice Self-Care

Being someone's emotional support system isn't always easy. No matter how much you care about someone else, you can't wear yourself down trying to help them.

Recharge your batteries if you're starting to feel drained. Include others your loved one may feel comfortable with if you start to feel too much is on your shoulders.

Do things to nurture yourself. Keep centered and replenish yourself. How do you do this?

Lee Harris, an inspiring intuitive messenger and transformational leader, says that when you are renewing yourself in situations like this, you also need to release the energy of others.

"So for example, to quickly direct a release and renewal, you might simply say: 'I release any energy and emotions which are not mine. I release any energy and emotions which are not mine.'"

This is like an energy detox. Let go of energy that depletes you. Being strong for others requires being strong for yourself first.

PUT YOUR OXYGEN MASK ON FIRST

There's a reason the safety instructions on airplanes tell you to put the oxygen mask on yourself first. You're no help to another if you're passed out or not breathing anymore.

Self-care is important for you too. When you need to rest and reboot, allow yourself that.

CHAPTER 16

They Remember Who Was There

I remember who was there for me when I really needed them.

I remember who listened, who heard me and who cared enough to pick up on non-verbal clues even I wasn't aware of. I especially remember the surprising supportive ones who showed up for me when I had no expectation that they would.

Little gestures mean a lot. Kindness in all forms has a healing power to it.

I remember every person who held me up with their emotional body weight when I could barely stand.

There is a special bond that forms when you share this kind of emotional intimacy and trust with another. These are the ones you remember and value for the rest of your life. These are very special people.

Part III: Grieving Community Forum

"The only people who think there's a time limit for grief, have never lost a piece of their heart. Take all the time you need."

— Unknown

CHAPTER 17

Kinship Through Loss

NOT A CLUB ANY OF US WANTED TO JOIN

People who lose their mother, especially those who were close to them, are in a club only they understand. They are among the few who can truly know what it does to a person.

They possess a special compassion for others going through the same experience.

Walking through grief can feel very lonely. Oftentimes, people in our life just can't appreciate what we are going through or they grow tired of hearing about the subject. Some may want us to *just get over it*" because they can't handle our pain and don't want to look at it.

You may learn to stifle your true feelings, just to make others more comfortable. As a result, you might feel even more misunderstood and alone.

No matter how hard we try, we simply cannot grieve according to other people's timelines.

THE POWER OF COMMUNITY

This is when joining a bereavement support group can often help. They are provided free of charge and require little commitment. The guidance and comfort they offer can be immensely beneficial.

Grief support groups can be found by contacting nearby hospitals, funeral homes, churches, synagogues and other places of worship. You might also find local Meetup support groups.

You can also simply go online and search for groups by typing in "grief support" or "bereavement groups" in your surrounding area.

There are also national organizations that provide useful resources as well as directories to free in-person, local grief support, including:

Hospice Foundation of America (www.HospiceFoundation.org)
American Hospice Foundation (www.AmericanHospice.org)
GriefShare (a biblical, Christ-based grief support ministry at www. Griefshare.org)
Grief.com (www.Grief.com)

When you connect with others going through the same experience, you can feel a true sense of community. You are given permission to speak more freely.

There's something healing that happens when you do: It helps you process faster. You might also gain valuable insights, advice, and understanding from others further along in their grief.

Most importantly, you see examples where people have made their way through this. That can help give you hope as you move forward.

But bereavement support groups aren't for everyone. Some individuals may be more private about sharing with a group of strangers. Others may feel too vulnerable and raw to be in the presence of others early in their own grief and grappling with the intense feelings of despair, sadness, anger, negativity, etc. It can feel overwhelming.

While community, comfort, and hope can be found in support groups, so can personality clashes, negativity and ill-informed advice. Each group will have its own personality.

If at first you don't succeed, keep trying a few others to see if you can find one better suited for you. It's most helpful if you look for a group that is focused on the loss of your mother—it keeps things more relatable.

It's important to remember that grief support groups can be an added resource. They are not a replacement for professional medical or psychological care.

ONLINE COMFORT

Just after my mom's death, I attended a few in-person support groups with mixed results. I kept trying different ones to see if I could find the right fit: One held at a hospital and another at a spiritual center both involved different kinds of losses and I didn't feel connected. Another local group left me depressed by so many people still deep in their grief even after years. Where was the hope I was searching for? I felt doomed.

Plus, I didn't always have the energy to get out of the house to attend in person. It's clear that grief doesn't wear a wristwatch or abide by any time schedule. It's nice to express your feelings when they surface, not put them on hold until the next scheduled meeting.

So I tried a few online bereavement groups, but one tailored to a mother's loss is what I felt would be most useful.

I formed *Healing After the Loss of Your Mother – Grief Support,* for others going through the same thing. People could come in and out as needed, get support or see what others were experiencing, share posts and get personal feedback, or just read through and not actively participate.

As the group grew, it was clear to all that despite the fact we come from diverse backgrounds, different countries, cultures, ages, genders, races, and beliefs, we all share one thing in common: We *know* just how hard it is to lose your mother.

This kind of grief is universal. It's intense. Together, we didn't feel so alone.

It's still important to be aware that online support groups can have the same downside as in-person ones. Both can be overwhelming at times. That's why it's key to take things at your own pace, check in and out when you need to, and enjoy the benefits of what a group experience can offer.

Besides a sense of community, being a support group member can also be uplifting when you see you've helped someone else just by sharing your experience or offering your own thoughts.

"Give what you can, take what you need," is a sentiment members in groups like this seem to share. That feels good. It's healing.

Instead of being alone and lost in the storm, you become a lighthouse for someone else.

CHAPTER 18

Community Commentary

If you're just joining the club—or supporting someone who is—you may wonder what it's like to be in a support group.

"What kinds of things do people in grief say and share?" "Would I relate?"

To experience the words of comfort shared among members and to hear different perspectives from people at various stages of the grieving process is to understand what "a sense of community" means.

One of the nicest surprises for me was to see how support group members—total strangers—really wrap their arms around each other through this healing process. We're all in it together.

COMMON THOUGHTS

(For privacy, names associated with the following comments have been omitted).

"You mean it's not just me?" It's a huge relief when you find you're not the only one going through a particular experience.

There are many common feelings that those in grief share. Here are just a few thoughts from people who've been there, to those just starting out:

"Sometimes, just having one person who understands and says, 'I get it,' helps."

"If you have never experienced this kind of pain, you probably won't understand it."

"It's comforting to talk to others so I see I'm not alone in my feelings. I'm not crazy."

"It really is true what they say. Our mothers teach us everything except for how to live without them."

"Life quickly becomes broken down into two segments: 'Life before mom died' and 'Life after mom died.' It's a marker that changes everything."

"I wouldn't wish this kind of pain on my worst enemy."

"I wonder when or if I'll ever regain my balance. I don't remember what it's like to feel 'normal' anymore. I just want to be there again."

"My husband and friends miss the old me. What they don't understand is I do, too."

"Unless I heard what other people are experiencing, I'd swear it was only me."

"I thought I had sustained major losses in my life until I lost my mom. That changes every single thing."

"We are all going through the loss of one, if not the only, true unconditional loves in our lives. It's a tremendous loss and that's why it hurts so much."

"Your mother's death has a way of making you see more clearly. Her love, not any annoyances or differences, is all that matters in the end. Maybe it's like childbirth where you forget about the pain. You just remember the love."

EXPERIENCE & ADVICE

When you've walked through grief, there is often a desire to help show others the way through. Here are some insights that may help light your path:

Q. What advice or tips do you have for those just starting out?

"Free grief counseling through hospice was very helpful to me in the beginning—it was my lifeline. Later, bereavement groups helped me from feeling less alone through this."

"New friends going through similar circumstances can be much more helpful sometimes than family."

"You can't go from devastation to happy overnight. It's a process. You'll get there."

"If someone reaches out to you, don't turn them away. Learn to accept and ask for help."

"This hard mourning period will pass. You will get stronger and the love for your mother will never fade. I wouldn't have believed it in the beginning."

"Don't just remember how she died… keep remembering how she lived."

"Try not to think about tomorrow. Worrying about the future can cause a great deal of added anxiety."

"Let yourself be sad, no one expects you to be happy at a time like this—it's perfectly normal."

"There were so many times I had to remember to just focus on only the very day, and sometimes down to the moment I was living in. The past and future can be depressing and scary sometimes, and there's nothing we can really do about either."

"Take one day, one hour at a time. Take small steps. If you get out of bed, shower, get dressed, and eat something, that's doing a lot in the beginning."

"It's okay to be sad. Just don't stay there."

"It wasn't easy going back to work, but having a focus and purpose does help."

"I cried rivers alone. I learned it was very helpful to just cry my eyes out randomly, daily and nightly. It is somehow healing."

"It's definitely not a linear process, not even a year out."

"When you begin to feel overwhelmed, 'Just do the next thing.' Baby steps can be big victories in moving gently forward."

"Be truthful, but careful with your words. I spoke some hurtful, angry words in the early weeks that I can't take back. Not everyone will accept your apology once you get more clear-headed."

"Keep going... don't give up even when it wears you down."

"You might be moving forward and something will stir things up again. It makes it real again. It's okay, it's just a slip. It's temporary."

"If you don't have something else to focus on, grief seems to be your default emotion for a long time."

"Try to acknowledge and just go with any feelings you may have. I stopped trying to run away from what was going on inside my heart. And then usually it's followed by a good, deep cry. I like a quote I found: 'Soap is to the body, what tears are to the soul.'"

"This is temporary. Remind yourself of this daily."

"You will always grieve, just differently than you do now. Differently than others do."

"If you're having trouble sleeping, like many of us, consider purchasing a weighted blanket. It's the one thing I found that really gives a feeling of security and helps me sleep through the night."

"When we lose our moms, we need somewhere else to place that love."

"Nothing can make me cry. It's a gift I give myself."

Throughout the day, make a conscious effort to see things to smile about."

"Grief never ends; it just becomes a part of who you are."

"Go through the grieving process, but give yourself permission to live again too."

"In the beginning, I truly felt like I was going crazy. It was unbearable. Something happens as time go on. Your heart will start healing slowly. Get through these days any way you can. Sometimes just taking a few minutes to sit quietly and breathe can bring some relief. You'll find moments of pleasure when you least expect them, eventually, they are more often. Get through a minute, an hour or a day at a time. We are all in this together."

POSITIVE CHANGES

Part of the grieving process includes not only the loss of your mother but also the loss of the old *you*. The process changes you, but as you rebuild, new positive attributes can develop.

Q. Have you changed throughout this process?

"I kept saying, 'I just want to feel normal again.' Grief does a makeover on all areas of your life. A year later, mine is simpler and more real now."

"It's amazing how your priorities change and you ditch the people who weren't there for you. You then form close bonds with people who go out of their way to help you."

"I'm finding a new voice and wisdom inside me. A new strength after going through this."

"You are never quite the same. A part of your heart goes with your mother. My goal, at first, was to recover the rest of my heart and focus some love on myself, my husband, my children, and grandchildren. It is harder than you think. My mind was so far away that it was like I was gone away too. The birth of my grandbabies helped me share love again."

"Grief has changed me completely, but not all of the ways in which it had, are for the worse. The worst has already happened in my life and that was losing her. I went through a period of time where I felt like I was so angry and hurt that nobody could hurt me ever again. So it has ultimately given me a confidence that I never had before."

"One positive change is that I've learned what is important in my life and what is not. Putting myself out there, having new experiences, making new memories with the new people that I meet along the way, that's what's important to me. In other words, living my life. I don't want to miss a second of it arguing anymore. It's stupid and a waste of precious time."

"I have become clearer about what works in my life and cleared the deck on what doesn't."

"I'm more appreciative of the fragility of life and I savor the sweetness so much more."

"In the beginning, I didn't know how I'd ever survive this pain. Now I see I'm stronger than I ever thought. I'm a survivor."

"I feel I became a more compassionate person."

"It has changed me. First I thought I'd never recover and would emerge a broken shell. I did stop functioning for a long while, but things have changed. I can see positives that have emerged. I'm more focused on my career and education. I'm no longer content with just plodding on! I have my drive back. I'm more forgiving. I really am thankful for the blessings that I do still have. I'm stronger than I ever thought possible! I can't believe I'm still standing to be honest. I'm changed and still feel broken and scared at times, but not all that's emerged is negative."

HINDSIGHT

Q: What are some things you know now that you wish you knew when you started?

"What a comforting fellowship there is in the grieving community."

"I think I was surprised by how many people are impatient with you and your grieving process, and how long it takes for you to get 'over it.' My mom died five years ago... I still grieve her."

"I had no idea how hard I was going to have to work to get back to myself. But I'm getting there."

"I didn't know that 'healing' could be so painful, but we do get through it."

"When I saw I wasn't the only one going through this, it allowed me to judge myself less and healing to begin."

"Trying to get used to the 'new me" is incredibly difficult and many people are puzzled and frustrated with this forced transformation."

"For one, I was surprised how all this would affect other people. Our family literally went crazy, including my husband who was very attached to my mom. He was unable to process his grief. He expressed it with a lot of anger, toward me and everyone, and it triggered a very severe mid-life crisis. I was not prepared for any of this. It took me a long time and grief counseling to understand the cause of all the turmoil was grief."

"It's not something to 'get over'. You just have to get through it or learn to live with it. Tomorrow is a year and I'm still knee deep in it."

"I was in denial for a really long time. With so much pain and so much going on in my life, it was just easier to pretend my mother was on a vacation or busy doing something. I was just delaying the inevitable and learned it will catch up with you sooner or later."

"I wish I knew earlier that everyone in my family would be grieving so differently. I expressed my pain and fell apart. One sibling was very stoic and kept it all in. We clashed as a result and it created a lot of conflict. I now see I mistook that as being cold and uncaring. It drove a wedge between us because we didn't have true understanding or compassion for what the other was feeling. We didn't want to be judged, but we judged the other. I now see that my sibling was processing a lot under the surface and was going through pain too."

"I wish I would have been able to prepare even slightly for the massive amount of pain that would come. I had no idea the amount of physical pain grief causes as well. I just wasn't prepared."

"I had no idea the depth of my sadness or the lack of words to describe what I'm feeling. There was so much exhaustion at the end of the work day and at the end of the week. I was just empty. I didn't know there'd be anxiety being around people that I know. I never realized how much energy chit-chat takes and I no longer have the desire or energy for it."

"I would have asked for more help early on and let everything out sooner."

"It can feel surreal for a very long time. To utter the words 'my mom is dead,' can stop you cold even years later. It feels unreal."

"I didn't believe the pain would ever stop, but it did."

The Time It Takes To Heal

Q: Does time really heal all wounds?

"I don't believe time itself heals anything, I believe we do. Time seems to lessen the pain, but heal it, not really. That's what we do as a gift to ourselves."

"I believe that grief becomes part of who you are. A new way of living with the loss."

"The greater the love, the greater the loss, the longer it will take to lessen the pain. In that sense, time does help."

"I personally don't think time alone can heal. I would wait for each day to end so I might be one day away from grief. It's not like that."

"Time alone doesn't. It's true that it really depends on what you do with the time."

"Time isn't a magic cure. I've been thinking about my mom a lot recently. She died more than 20 years ago and it's just kicking in now. I think I was stuck in some sort of denial for ages."

"Not really. I went to work 10 days after my mom passed and no one seemed to understand why I wasn't acting like myself. Several people even said to me, 'I'll be glad when you get back to how you used to be.' Sorry guys, that person is gone."

"I'm sending my eldest daughter off to college tomorrow and this opens up all my grief again over losing my mother. My mom died 14 years ago and I'm missing her so much right now. There are so many things I want to ask her. The separation I'm feeling with my own daughter leaving magnifies the separation I feel about my mom dying."

"Grief doesn't care about time. It can wait. It's only been 10 months. I had to 'shelf' my grief for work and I forgot how to take it back off. I didn't really want to feel the pain, but now it's back with a vengeance."

"My Mom was my best friend and I loved her more than I can even describe. I thought I was literally going to die when she died. For a few months, it was like that. I felt I couldn't handle the pain. But it's been over 6 months now and I have to say that time, therapy, patience, and support groups have helped a lot. Time doesn't heal the fact that I miss her and that I sometimes feel sad when I think of her, but time has helped me get through a lot of the pain. I hope it helps you too."

Part IV: The Way Forward

"When you walk through a storm
Hold your chin up high
And don't be afraid of the dark.
At the end of a storm
Is a golden sky
And the sweet, silver song of a lark.
Walk on, through the wind,
Walk on, through the rain,
Though your dreams be tossed and blown.
Walk on, walk on with hope in your heart,
And you'll never walk alone,
You'll never walk alone."

— "You'll Never Walk Alone" lyrics (from
"Carousel") Oscar Hammerstein II,
Richard Rodgers, Songwriters

CHAPTER 19

Moving Forward is Not Moving On

The one thing I didn't realize in the beginning was that grief never really ends.

It will ease over time. You will create a new way of living and find your new normal.

There will be days when you no longer think about your mother's death all the time or find yourself in profound pain.

It is essential to remember that when the hurt softens and you begin to get back on your emotional feet, you will not *move on*, you will simply *move forward.*

DOES HEALING MEAN LETTING HER GO?

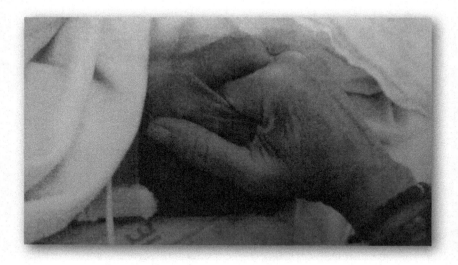

You will never let your mom go. She is a part of you.

One of my biggest fears—and a common one—was that if I let go of my grief, I might somehow be letting go of my mom.

It felt like grief was the last thread that still connected us. It showed me she lived. That she mattered.

My fear was that if I released that, I'd be releasing her. I didn't want to lose her all over again.

That's not the case and never will it be. The soulbond between mother and child will always be there.

With the passage of time, I still think about her almost as often—just not with as much sadness anymore.

There will be a day when your heart isn't feeling so broken. You can then tell the pain, "Hush. You can go now." That's when you create more space for peaceful memories to find their way back in.

When that day comes, you will find her there and your heart connection still strong.

Give yourself time.

FED UP WITH BEING SAD

You know you've finally turned a corner when you wake up one day and decide you've had enough.

Your mind and your body are exhausted. You just don't want to be in pain anymore.

Michael Beckwith, founder of the Agape International Spiritual Center in Los Angeles, California, phrased it well: "It is said that suffering is the great awakener. Many times we must hit bottom and experience great pain, which then becomes the impetus for genuine transformation."

I thought to myself, "I don't want to feel sad anymore." I wanted some form of my life back. That was my wake up moment.

Or maybe it was my mom whispering after a long sleep, "Come on, Honey. It's time to get up." That's what it can feel like on a soul level: an awakening.

INTENTION TO HEAL

Throughout all of this, remember you have a choice.

If you want to feel better, begin by having a simple intention that you want to feel better. That's no small step; that really is a giant leap for your heart.

THE POWER OF NOW

Eckhart Tolle famously teaches that the now is all we really have. The past is over. The future hasn't happened yet. All we really have is the present moment.

He says making the Now your primary focus in life, becoming aware of your thinking, and not identifying with your pain is the way to happiness.

In his book *The Power of Now: A Guide to Spiritual Enlightenment,* Tolle writes, "Let me summarize the process. Focus your attention on the feeling inside you. Know that it is the pain-body. Accept that it is there. Don't *think* about it – don't let the feeling turn into thinking. Don't judge or analyze. Don't make an identity for yourself out of it. Stay present, and continue to be the observer of what is happening inside you. Become aware not only of the emotional pain but also of 'the one who observes,' the silent watcher. This is the power of the Now, the power of your own conscious presence."

BE AWARE OF YOUR THOUGHTS

Becoming more mindful of your thoughts is key. Don't let your mental chatter drive the bus. Take the wheel.

You don't have to be polite and give all your thoughts your attention.

In the book *Ask and It Is Given: Learning to Manifest Your Desire,* Esther and Jerry Hicks teach about how, with practice, you can become a joyful, deliberate creator.

"As you consciously consider the way you feel, you will get better and better at directing the Source Energy, and you will become a disciplined and joyous *deliberate creator*," they write. "With practice, you will be able to achieve a focused control of this *Creative Energy*, and, like the skilled sculptor, you will take delight in the molding of the Energy, which creates worlds, and direct it toward your individual creative endeavors."

MOMENTUM

When you become more deliberate in what you think about, you will see how they can build momentum in either direction.

You have a choice. If you want to feel better, keep reaching for better feeling thoughts. Keep pointing in the direction that feels good and offers relief.

This will help shape your experience for the better. The more you focus, the more of those thoughts you get.

Using this basic principle of The Law of Attraction is simple to apply and is very effective.

Positive momentum helps you regain your balance, build emotional strength, and have a feeling of well-being. It helps you find your way back to *you* again.

ACCEPTANCE IS NOT WHAT YOU THINK

As a society, we're taught *acceptance* is the last stage of grief—the end point and goal. Many struggle with the whole concept.

As mentioned earlier in this book, the misunderstanding of the five stages of grief has left many with a lot of anxiety that they are somehow "doing it wrong" or failing in the process if they can't get there.

"I can't imagine how I can ever *accept* that my mom is dead," was me weeks after my mother's death, echoing what so many others say after a loss this big.

I could accept the reality that she died. I would adjust. I wasn't in denial, but I couldn't imagine ever being "at peace" with the reality of her death. I couldn't see how I could ever be "okay with it."

That stage just never made sense to me.

Certified grief coach, Tamaara Smith clarifies this widely held misconception: "Acceptance doesn't mean we actually *like* what has occurred, it simply means we are no longer fighting the *reality* of what has actually happened."

Acceptance doesn't mean that "I'm okay with the fact my mom is dead." Rather, "My mom is dead, but I accept this sad reality."

CHAPTER 20

The Way Toward Happiness

Getting a sense of *you* back takes time. It starts when you come to terms with the fact that life has changed, but you will go on. You start to learn to adjust.

There is a transformational period to go through as you let go of your old self and identity, and birth a new *you*.

A combination of the passage of time and actively processing your feelings helps your emotions settle and level off. The good days begin to outweigh the bad, and you begin to smile a little more. You engage more with life, and your desire for social interaction comes back online.

This is when you open yourself more to life and happiness. It's the way forward. You're not just ready, you're doing it!

CHANGE HAPPENS

Change really is the only constant in life. I guess that's what *surrender* is all about.

Cindy Bentley, an international energy practitioner, *Reiki* master & dowser, former registered nurse of 37 years, and author of the book *Celestial Being: How to Shift to Fifth Dimensional Living* offers some words of insight and comfort: "There is no permanence here, only change. In each moment, you must decide how you will be, what you will be or who you will become. How you meet this moment is formed from your level of self-awareness."

She explains that when we experience a lot of change, moving forward means leaving our old self and feelings of security in the world behind. We need to give ourselves time to grieve that loss and adjust.

"It's okay to give yourself permission to be in pain," she says. It's naturally sad to realize you are not the same as you were and never will be.

"There's no permanence, as much as we want things to be stable and good and comfortable. That just isn't the way life works," Bentley adds.

I'm not a big fan of change—okay, I'm a recovering control freak—and death is the biggest change agent of all. Losing a sense of security and turning my world upside down really knocked me for a loop.

Learning to accept the fact that *change happens* is a helpful step toward healing.

Release Expectations

Another piece of good advice that Bentley offers is that in order to move forward and heal, we need to let go of expectations of who we were, where we thought we were going, and how life would be. Ask yourself: "What is holding me back? What needs to be released?"

We experience pain, she explains, when our expectations have not been met. Breathe deeply, give yourself permission to cry and release the old you as you embrace the new.

ACCEPTING WHAT IS

You don't need to like any aspect of reality to accept *it is what it is.*

In *The Power of Now*, Tolle reminds us, "Always say 'yes' to the present moment. What could be more futile, more insane, than to create an inner resistance to something that already is?" he writes. "Surrender to what *is*. Say 'yes' to life – and see how life suddenly starts working *for* you rather than against you."

THE WAY THROUGH

Tolle goes on to write, "Accepting the pain of your suffering and allowing yourself the space to grieve will give you peace and within that peace, you will find joy once again."

Time and surrender can be your two best friends here.

The way through is about embracing change, releasing expectations and accepting the adjusted realties involving:

* Your mom's physical loss.
* Your life structure.
* Changes in you.

You mourn the loss of *a lot* through this. This all takes a while to settle in, but it's the way out of grief.

CHAPTER 21

The Path To Healing

LEANING FORWARD

Ultimately, you heal through grief, not from it. You walk through it.
It's sometimes messy and there's no predictability to the process.
You may lose people along the way as your priorities change.
You will see who is there for you when you really need them
and who is not. Through this, you'll tighten the circle of people
you can count on and you'll value those people like never before.

This experience has a way of bringing into focus what matters
and what doesn't. It gives you a new perspective. You will recognize
who and what really matters in your life and let go of what doesn't.

You evolve through grief. It's all a cleansing and healing process and it's your own.

FINAL THOUGHT

Grief can make you grow in ways you weren't prepared for. Your
pain and scars can make you more compassionate, more vulnerable, stronger, and wiser.

A richer appreciation for life develops. You gain simple clarity. Ultimately, death can bring a deeper meaning to life.

My friend's assurance, "You will survive this" is true. You will.

But survival isn't about one final destination: It's about getting through each moment, each day, each year, and each bumpy emotion that surfaces throughout a lifetime.

It's about facing whatever comes up and getting through it. It's about adapting to change and embracing life again.

That's survival. That's how we heal. It happens slowly, but it happens... one step at a time.

You've got this.

MESSAGE FROM THE AUTHOR

I know this isn't an easy road. I wish you peace and comfort in the days, weeks and months ahead.

Be easy with yourself and with the process.

Surround yourself with loving, heart-centered, understanding people. Reach out even to strangers; you'll be surprised as to how much compassion is out there when it comes to this subject.

Above all, please know I wish you love and healing.

ABOUT THE AUTHOR

Elaine Mallon's insight into grief comes from the devastating experience of losing her own mother. She knows the magnitude of this heartbreak firsthand. Elaine tried to channel her loss in a way that might provide comfort to others and bring meaning to her own experience.

It was her mother, Irma, who nurtured Elaine's love of writing as a child and encouraged her to follow her passion as an adult.

A couple years before she died, Elaine's mom gave her a copy of "Chicken Soup For the Writer's Soul: Stories to Open the Heart and Rekindle the Spirit of Writers" for Christmas.

She never stopped encouraging Elaine's writing in all forms. Just after her mother's death, Elaine picked up the book and felt her mom telling her it was time to write. With deep empathy for those who might feel lost, misunderstood or alone after the loss of their mother, Elaine felt compelled to write the grief recovery guidebook she desperately needed when her own mom died.

Elaine is an award-winning public relations and marketing veteran who began her professional career in entertainment publicity where she was a publicist for MGM/UA Television and

CBS Television, and later became Vice President, Media & Corporate Relations at 20th Century Fox Television.

She currently lives in Los Angeles. In addition to writing, Elaine established Healing After The Loss of Your Mother – Grief Support, an online group and sacred space for those seeking comfort & community through their loss.

For more information, visit: www.HealingAfterTheLossOfYour Mother.com

Elaine Mallon, Author

My mom, Irma Mallon.

The Suicide Prevention Lifeline: www.suicidepreventionlifeline.
   org
International Association for Suicide Prevention:
www.Iasp.info
Hospice Foundation of America: www.hospicefoundation.org

American Hospice Foundation: www.americanhospice.org
What's Your Grief blog: www.whatsyourgrief.com
Griefshare: www.griefshare.org
Griefshare.com: www.grief.com
Grief.com: www.grief.com
Grief Healing Blog: www.griefhealingblog.com
Mayo Clinic: www.mayoclinic.org
Harvard Health Medical Newsletter: www.health.harvard.edu
National Institute of Mental Health: www.nimh.nih.gov
Psychology Today: www.psychologytoday.com
YouTube: www.youtube.com
Cindy Bentley: www.dnareconnection.com
Brené Brown: www.brenebrown.com
Lee Harris: www.leeharrisenergy.com
Michael Lennox: www.michaellennox.com
Karen Hager: www.karenhager.com
Michael Beckwith: www.agapelive.com
TheGrievingMind.com: www.thegrievingmind.com

Dennis, Rebecca. *And Breathe: The Complete Guide to Conscious Breathing for Health & Happiness.* London: Orion Publishing Group, 2016.

Hicks, Esther, and Jerry. *Ask and It Is Given: Learning To Manifest Your Desires.* Carlsbad: Hay House, Inc., 2004

Hicks, Esther, and Jerry. *The Law of Attraction: The Basics of the Teachings of Abraham.* Carlsbad: Hay House, Inc., 2006

Kubler-Ross, Elizabeth, and Kessler, David. *On Grief & Grieving: Finding the Meaning of Grief Through the Five Stages of Loss.* New York: Simon & Schuster, 2005.

Pennebaker, James W., PhD. *Writing to Heal: A Guided Journal for Recovering from Trauma and Emotional Upheaval.* Oakland: New Harbinger Publications, 2004.

Tolle, Eckhart. *The Power of Now: A Guide to Spiritual Enlightenment.* Canada: Namaste Publishing, 1997.

Tolle, Eckhart. *A New Earth: Awakening to Your Life's Purpose.* New York: A Plume Book, 2006.

Orloff, Judith. *Emotional Healing: Liberate Yourself from Negative Emotions and Transform Your Life.* New York: Harmony, 2010.

Worden, William. *Grief Counseling and Grief Therapy: A Handbook for the Mental Health Practitioner, Fifth Edition.* New York: Springer, 2018.

YOUR PERSONAL JOURNALING SECTION

"Be the silent watcher of your thoughts and behavior. You are beneath the thinker. You are the stillness beneath the mental noise. You are the love and joy beneath the pain."

— Eckhart Tolle

Your private journaling pages are here if you need them:

- Notes To Myself
- Favorite Stories & Memories
- Gratitude Journal

Notes To Myself:

Use this section to write down things you found helpful, important points to remember, random thoughts, dreams you may have, signs you may get or milestones worth noting.

Write on...

_____

_____

_____

_____

_____

_____

_____

_____

_____

_____

_____

_____

_____

_____

_____

_____

_____

_____

_____

_____

_____

_____

_____

"A good life is a collection of happy moments."

— Denis Waitley

FAVORITE STORIES & MEMORIES:

Memories bring the past to the present moment. What happy memory or stories do you have about your mother that makes you smile?

Jot down anything that's heartwarming or funny that you can remember.

It great to re-read this section when you are missing your mom. It's also nice to share these memories with others.

Use a favorite picture of her to bookmark this section if you need to. She'll always be here.

_____

_____

_____

*"Appreciating what shows up in your life
changes your personal vibration. Gratitude
elevates your life to a higher frequency."*

— Oprah Winfrey

GRATITUDE JOURNAL

Gratitude is the art of being thankful. Anything—big or small—
that gives you a positive feeling is worth writing down.

In good times and bad, it's important to look for the light. The
more you look, the more you'll find.

If you're feeling down, you can read through this section again.
It will be *you...* comforting you.

_____

_____

_____

_____

_____

Elaine Mallon

_____

_____

_____

_____

_____

_____

_____

_____

_____

_____

_____

_____

_____

_____

_____

_____

_____

_____

_____

_____

_____

#